I was raised by good people who believed that if the King James Version was good enough for Jesus, it was good enough for us. For lots of good reasons, we've learned to read and trust other translations. But I'm grateful to Jon Sweeney for helping us remember the text that inspired so many saints, the language that we once held in common, and—most importantly—the strange speech that reminded people for centuries that the King's English was 'contemporary' and that we are always aliens and strangers in this world.

Jonathan Wilson-Hartgrove

—

Jon Sweeney, one of my favorite contemporary spiritual writers, turns his considerable talents to the story of the world's best-known translation of the world's best-known book: The King James Bible. By recounting its fascinating history, showing the superlative beauty of its prose, describing its lasting effect on individual believers, and even pointing out its occasional, if inadvertent, humor (e.g., "He stinketh"), Sweeney will make you love a beloved translation even more. If you're looking for a good guide to understanding the KJV, as its translators would undoubtedly say: 'Verily, thou hast found the right man.'"

James Martin, SJ
author of the *New York Times* bestseller
The Jesuit Guide to (Almost) Everything

Also by Jon Sweeney

The Road to Assisi (editor)

Born Again and Again

The St. Francis Prayer Book

Light in the Dark Ages

Ireland's Saint (editor)

Almost Catholic

Cloister Talks

Verily, Verily

THE KJV – 400 YEARS OF INFLUENCE AND BEAUTY

JON SWEENEY

ZONDERVAN®

ZONDERVAN.com/
AUTHORTRACKER
follow your favorite authors

ZONDERVAN

Verily, Verily
Copyright © 2011 by Jon Sweeney

This title is also available as a Zondervan ebook. Visit www.zondervan.com/ebooks.

This title is also available in a Zondervan audio edition. Visit www.zondervan.fm.

Requests for information should be addressed to:

Zondervan, *Grand Rapids, Michigan 49530*

Library of Congress Cataloging-in-Publication Data

Sweeney, Jon M., 1967-
    Verily, verily : the KJV: 400 years of influence and beauty / Jon Sweeney.
        p.   cm.
    ISBN 978-0-310-32025-8 (hardcover, jacketed)
    1. Bible. English. Authorized—History. 2. Bible. English. Authorized—Influence. I.
Title.
BS186.S94 2011
220.520309—dc22   2010037272

Published in association with the literary agency of Daniel Literary Group, LLC, 1701 Kingsbury Drive, Suite 100, Nashville, TN 37215.

Cover design: *Juicebox Designs*
Interior design: *Katherine Lloyd*
Editing: *Robert R. Hudson*

Printed in the United States of America

11 12 13 14 15 /DCI/ 24 23 22 21 20 19 18 17 16 15 14 13 12 11 10 9 8 7 6 5 4 3 2 1

To the dedicated Sunday school teachers
Who made sure we knew John 3:16 and Psalm 23
In the King's English

CONTENTS

AUTHOR'S NOTE

When I quote the King James Version of the Bible (KJV), I am quoting from the original 1611 edition, but without the old spellings. A landmark of Early Modern English, the KJV nevertheless retained more Middle English spellings than we're used to today. Throw that together with old typographic conventions like the interchanging *v* and *u* (the character *u* being used for the *v* sound inside a word, and the character *v* being used for the *u* sound at the beginnings of words), and the original KJV can be downright disorienting. For example, consider this sentence from the narrative of the flood: "And behold I, euen I, doe bring a flood of waters vpon the earth." Ever since the 1769 Oxford Standard Edition, modern spelling has been used: "And, behold, I, even I, do bring a flood of waters upon the earth." I also use spellings that tend to reflect English usage in the United States, rather than in the United Kingdom. So, for example, in my title to chapter 4, when I quote from the translators' preface of the 1611 KJV, I write, "Lo, the Humor!" rather than, "Lo, the Humour!"

Since its beginning, the KJV has also italicized a lot of words to indicate that those are implied but not actually present in the original languages. These are called "provided words." More about that in chapter 3. I find that such italicizing is no longer necessary — so that has also been discarded here.

Above all, my desire is that *Verily, Verily* will inspire people to return to the text of the King James Bible. I hope that it leads you to read it again — or for the first time.

BURYING AND RESURRECTING BIBLES

As the hart panteth after the water brooks,
so panteth my soul after thee, O God.
PSALM 42:1

That instant was I turned into a hart,
And my desires, like fell and cruel hounds,
E'er since pursue me.
SHAKESPEARE, *TWELFTH NIGHT*, ACT 1, SCENE 1

I've buried quite a few Bibles in the last decade. At our church in Vermont, I'm in charge of the annual book sale. Donations pour in over a six-week period, and I weed through them all, sorting, pricing, and packing them into cartons, where they wait until the fair on the Village Green.

Each year we receive about a dozen Bibles, nearly all of which are the King James Version. They always appear well-worn, with tattered edges on the old leather covers. Often, the leather is so old and dry that it chips like paint on the side of a weathered shed. Looking at these donated Bibles, I imagine that they've

11

been cleaned out of attics or assisted-care facilities. Many of our grandmothers and grandfathers read KJVs exclusively, marking them and urging us to read them when we were young. They recorded important dates in this marvelous book, also known as "The Authorized Version." Senator Sam Ervin of North Carolina (1896-1985) put it best when he said:

> I think that the greatest book, from a literary as well as from a religious standpoint ever made available to mankind, is the King James Version of the Bible. As soon as my forebears obtained the [KJV], they adopted it as a guide for their religious faith, and they recorded within its covers their marriages, their births, and their deaths. They found something within that old Book which revealed to them the promises of God, and something which made them fear God and nothing else.[1]

I once asked an antique dealer in town where he obtained all of the KJVs in his shop. He said matter-of-factly, "There's a Bible in every house." Bibles were once among the most treasured objects in a family home, but a KJV no longer seems important. At our book fair, I hear things like, "Mother kept this by her bedside for as long as I can remember. But we don't need it."

With all the new translations available, old King James Bibles are rarely appreciated—but they are, nevertheless, essential cultural artifacts. The KJV has something to say about who we are. As recently as the 1990s, President Bill Clinton used the King James Bible given to him by his grandmother for his inaugural oaths. It was open to this verse at the 1993 ceremony:

---

1. Sam Ervin, *The Wisdom of Sam Ervin* (New York: Ballantine Books, 1973), 121.

For he that soweth to his flesh shall of the flesh reap corruption; but he that soweth to the Spirit shall of the Spirit reap life everlasting.

GALATIANS 6:8

And at the second inauguration, it was open to this:

And they that shall be of thee shall build the old waste places: thou shalt raise up the foundations of many generations; and thou shalt be called, The repairer of the breach, The restorer of paths to dwell in.

ISAIAH 58:12[2]

In 1989, President George H. W. Bush used one — the "Washington Bible" — first used by George Washington at his inauguration in 1789. And in 2009, Barack Obama became the first U.S. president to reuse the Bible on which Abraham Lincoln placed his hand at his inauguration in 1861. Honest Abe's was a KJV too!

But today, most of the King James Bibles I come across are battered and ragged, well-used and dusty. At our book fair, no one wants to buy them. I usually can't even give them away.

So I end up burying a lot of Bibles. That's what you're supposed to do with no-longer-needed holy books. At the end of the fair in late July, I carry the leftovers home and get the tall shovel out of the shed. Using the heel of my right shoe, I thrust its blade deep into the soil and make a hole large enough for a dead pet. In they go.

In fact, each of the three monotheistic faiths practice some form of this. There are a series of underground tunnels in the Chiltan Hills near Quetta, Pakistan, where nearly 100,000 discarded and

---

2. Information compiled for the Architect of the Capitol, a U.S. government agency serving Congress. As of August 2010, this information was available online at memory.loc.gov/ammem/pihtml/pibible.html#notes.

partial Qur'ans are carefully packed in bags, buried (which they actually call "storing," in a hopeful sort of way), and then watched over by devout Muslims who feel called to the sacred task. The first of these many tunnels was dug in 1992 and measures 130 feet in length, and is about seven feet in circumference.[3]

On a much less impressive scale, someday someone will buy my old house, dig up the rear part of the garden (look to the area closest to the shed, near the remnants of last year's tomato plants), and likely scratch their heads at what they find about twenty-two inches down.

A RICH HERITAGE

For the last two decades, I have attended an Episcopalian church. Episcopalians — like Christians in many other denominations and churches — aren't really supposed to read the King James Version anymore. It's almost embarrassing to tell someone that you read the KJV. It can feel like admitting that your favorite television show is still *Mutual of Omaha's Wild Kingdom*. If it were to be spied on a table during a dinner party, a guest might assume that the attic had recently been cleaned.

But I grew up with King James language — I breathed it like air. I memorized long passages that remain with me. As a kid, I rarely said anything worth repeating, but when I did, my mother would remark to my father, "Out of the mouth of babes" (Psalm 8:2). Today, I can no more unhinge some of these phrases and verses from my psyche than I can go back in time and undo the mistakes that I made in high school.

---

3. They are a registered charity with the Pakistani government called Jabal-e-Noor-ul-Quran Quetta, which as of August 2010 had an active Facebook page and a registered website, jnqqta.org, that wasn't working.

My Baptist grandfathers—of the old school, both of them—believed, for doctrinal reasons, that nothing should replace the KJV. They thought it represented a pure moment in the history of human connection to God. Both preachers, they had fat, black KJV study Bibles, which they shook in their hands while they preached from behind their pulpits. Alister McGrath, one of today's finest historians, says, "It can be argued that, until the end of the First World War, the King James Bible was seen, not simply as the most important English translation of the Bible, but as one of the finest literary works in the English language."[4]

I still love the cadences and language of the KJV, though I cannot agree that the newer translations are deficient or unfaithful to the original text. In fact, I know the exact opposite is usually true. The New Revised Standard Version (NRSV) seems to be the preferred translation of today's academics because of its contemporary scholarship, use of the most recent manuscripts—including those discovered among the Dead Sea Scrolls—removal of archaisms, attention to the differences between genres (typesetting poetry as poetry, presenting the Song of Songs as drama, and so on), and the use of appropriate gender-inclusive language. But of course there are many others. For example, I know that the New International Version (NIV) and Today's New International Version (TNIV) are preferred by many pastors, and quite a few poets and writers are partial to the Revised English Bible (REB).

But the KJV is the only one that is a building block of our collective cultural heritage. It is like the characters in Dickens or the speeches of Martin Luther King Jr. (both fans of the KJV). Where would we be without phrases like these?

---

4. Alister McGrath, *In the Beginning: The Story of the King James Bible and How It Changed a Nation, a Language, and a Culture* (New York: Doubleday, 2001), 3.

the fat of the land
eat, drink, and be merry
the apple of his eye
an eye for an eye
it came to pass
fight the good fight
fell flat on his face
the fullness of time
can a leopard change his spots?
am I my brother's keeper?[5]

just to name a few.

Phrases from the King James Bible have explained subtle life lessons to us over and over again in ways that are irreplaceable. It's not necessarily that these expressions are *better* than those in other Bible translations, but that they have formed the minds and hearts of more English-speakers than any other translation. For example:

God's care for us: "The LORD is my shepherd"
Freedom from slavery: "Let my people go"
A life wasted in worries over unimportant things: "Vanity
    of vanities"
A self-righteous person: "Holier than thou"
Work that you adore: "A labor of love"
A metaphor for being good in the world: "The salt of the
    earth"
A metaphor against in-fighting: a "house divided against
    itself shall not stand"

---

5. These well-known KJV phrases are from, respectively, Genesis 45:18, Luke 12:19, Deuteronomy 32:10, Matthew 5:38, Genesis 38:27, 1 Timothy 6:12, Numbers 22:31, Galatians 4:4 (as well as Ephesians 1:10), Jeremiah 13:23, Genesis 4:9

Our relationship to truth: "We see through a glass, darkly"
What CNN will say when a politician's dirty secrets are
    revealed: "How are the mighty fallen"
A really close call: by "the skin of my teeth."[6]

Bible scholars tell us that many phrases from the KJV were actually culled from William Tyndale's version, published about eighty-five years earlier.[7] In that previous century, Tyndale was burned at the stake because he dared to upstage God's Latin, translating the Scripture's original Hebrew and Greek into the King's English. So let's give William his due for "filthy lucre" (1 Timothy 3:3), "the spirit indeed is willing, but the flesh is weak" (Matthew 26:41), "Am I my brother's keeper?" (Genesis 4:9), "fell flat on his face" (Numbers 22:31), and the best of all, "In him we live, and move, and have our being" (Acts 17:28). The wise KJV translation committees retained each of these.

Other phrases, such as "the patience of Job" (James 5:11), required no special innovation, but only straightforward translation, and yet they are phrases that—from William Tyndale to the King James Bible to us—long ago entered our everyday speech.

THE THEES AND THE THOUS

I know what you may be thinking: Okay ... maybe so ... but all those obscure, ancient words and phrases get in the way! *Behold ... forasmuch ... thence*—enough already! Is this true—do the Jacobean

---

6. These are from, respectively, Psalm 23:1, Exodus 5:1, Ecclesiastes 1:2 (and12:8), Isaiah 65:5, 1 Thessalonians 1:3, Matthew 5:13, Matthew 12:25, 1 Corinthians 13:12, 2 Samuel 1:27, Job 19:20

7. David Daniell, *Tyndale's New Testament* (New Haven, Conn.: Yale University Press, 1989), vii.

adverbs and pronouns keep us from hearing what the text has to say? I hope not.

Just as reading Shakespeare's *King Lear* can be difficult, so can reading the KJV. Our language has changed quite a bit in the last four hundred years. Or think about it another way: the same phrases that are difficult in the KJV can also be part of its charm. The setting, context, and language of another era can yield rich color and nuance to what might otherwise seem more ordinary. Lo, verily verily, whoso!

Contemporary English translations make the Word of God accessible, but they can also make it seem ordinary. In their attempt to be faithful to the Hebrew and Greek originals, the translators of the KJV sometimes even chose language that was a bit odd by the standards of their day. Unlike Tyndale before them, they didn't always aim for what we might call "contemporary English." Accessibility wasn't their only intention. To reach people who feel that what the Bible has to say is already alien to their experience, Tyndale, as well as most Bible publishers today, often use language that's made to read like a popular novel. There doesn't seem to be much evidence that these strategies have worked to find more readers, however.[8] Does the average adult know the Bible better today, for instance, with our dozens of contemporary English translations, than a similar adult may have, say, 150 years ago?

From its beginnings, the KJV was somewhat old-fashioned and classic. Its language and syntax were not always grounded in the spoken language of the day but were instead more literary. We see

---

8. One notable exception was the first publication of the complete *Living Bible*, paraphrased (not translated from the original languages) by Kenneth N. Taylor, who was at that time director of Moody Press in Chicago. It was first published in 1971 and amazingly became the bestselling book (not just Bible or religious book) in the United States in both 1972 and 1973.

this in the way that the translators usually steered away from *you* for the second-person plural (nominative), using only *ye* instead. Also, the KJV used only *thee* and *thou* for the singular, even though *you* had become a common singular form by the time of King James. *Ye*, *thee*, and *thou* carried a bit of literary flair and lent more music to the KJV than was present in some of the earlier English vernacular Bibles. For these reasons, some scholars have called the KJV "a deliberate piece of social and linguistic engineering."[9]

The English language changed more rapidly in the 160 years between the invention of the printing press (around 1450) and the publication of the KJV (1611), than it had before or it has since. Our translators responded to this change by seeking to imitate some of the rhythms and cadences of the Vulgate — the Latin classic that no vernacular English Bible had yet truly displaced — to help create a bridge to this new effort intended to become the authorized standard in all English churches. The translators wanted the KJV's first readers to feel that they were still reading the very words of God — even though those words were now offered in English. Those early seventeenth-century translators seemed to understand that there's an integrity to what is venerably classic, and the larger the gap between what's smoothly understood and what's somewhat more challenging is sometimes all that separates what is to be easily passed over from what is of enduring use and value.

At the same time, they were able to create a vernacular Bible that was self-consciously a *translation*, in contrast to common medieval attitudes toward the Vulgate. As one scholar has explained this, "For the man of the Middle Ages the Latin Bible, which had been in continuous use by the Western Church since St. Jerome

---

9. *The Bible: Authorized King James Version*, Robert Carroll and Stephen Prickett, eds. (New York: Oxford University Press, 2008), xxviii.

translated it … quite simply *was* the Bible. But the first thing the reader of the Authorized Version comes across, after the Epistle of Dedication to the King, is an essay entitled 'The Translator to the Reader.'"[10] More on this to come.

I have found that the beauty of the old language shines most when it is spoken aloud, rather than read only in the mind. (Silent, private reading is mostly a modern invention anyway.) *Thee, thou, thy,* and *thine* will always sound more appropriately reverent to my modern ear as pronouns for God, than will *you* and *your* (even though the *thee* and *thou* forms were actually the intimate, personal forms of address in King James's time). God is magnificent and diverse and so should be God's pronouns. In my church, we usually repeat the following verse from the KJV after a collection has been taken: "All things come of thee, and of thine own have we given thee" (1 Chronicles 29:14). I much prefer it over the NRSV rendering, "For all things come from you, and of your own have we given you."

There are hundreds of similar examples — of when the language and spirit of the KJV rings true — that I will share with you in the coming chapters.

So the next time you are cleaning out an elderly loved one's attic, give the KJV another try. If you spend the next two hundred or so pages with me, I will show you why this old original is a way for you to discover the Word of God in the form in which it's changed more lives than any other Bible in history. You will see why people were willing to die in order to create the first English vernacular Bibles. You might hear echoes of the speeches of Abraham Lincoln, Dr. King, or even Gandhi. You may find yourself

---

10. Gabriel Josipovici, *The Book of God: A Response to the Bible* (New Haven: Yale University Press, 1990), 32.

writing in the margins and memorizing some of the great phrases and verses that earlier generations of Christians did. I pray that your cup will, for a time, "runneth over" rather than "overflow" (Psalm 23:5)!

INTRODUCTION

In the beginning was the Word,
and the Word was with God,
and the Word was God. . . . In him was life;
and the life was the light of men.

JOHN 1:1, 4

Word. Noun, singular.
"The second person of the ever adorable Trinity."

DR. SAMUEL JOHNSON

I recently conducted an extremely unscientific survey of Christians. I wanted to test what we can identify as language that originated with the King James Bible. So I asked five different groups — each of twenty or so church-going people, representing several denominations, in different parts of the country — to look at the following list of phrases and answer this question: Did this originate with the KJV? (And just to be clear, I informed my quiz-takers that I wasn't slipping in any phrases from Tyndale or other translations. So, in effect, I was asking them: Is this phrase from the Bible?)

From the King James Bible or some other source? Identify the origin of the following phrases or sentences from English literature. Simply answer "KJV" or "not KJV."

Which are from the KJV?

1. There is method to my
   madness.

2. Love is strong as death.

3. In the twinkling of an eye.

4. A plague on both your
   houses.

5. Gave up the ghost.

6. We turn not older with
   years, but newer every day.

7. The wisdom of Solomon.

8. As pure as the driven
   snow.

Here are the answers.

1. Not KJV. This phrase is
   actually inspired by the
   words of the character,
   Polonius, in Shakespeare's
   Hamlet: "Though this
   be madness, yet there is
   method in it."

2. Song of Solomon 8:6

3. 1 Corinthians 15:52

4. Not KJV: Shakespeare,
   Romeo and Juliet.

5. John 19:30

6. Not KJV: Emily Dickinson.

7. Matthew 12:42

8. Shakespeare again. His
   writings are probably second
   to the KJV in sources for
   popular English idioms,
   including "hobnob" and
   "wear my heart upon
   my sleeve." This one is
   a combination of two
   different quotations: "as
   white as driven snow,"
   from *The Winter's Tale,* and
   "black Macbeth will seem as
   pure as snow," in *Macbeth.*

9. Better to remain silent and be thought a fool than to speak out and remove all doubt.

9. Not KJV: Abraham Lincoln.

10. O ye of little faith.

10. Luke 12:28

11. A cloud of witnesses.

11. Hebrews 12:1

12. If you tell the truth, you don't have to remember anything.

12. Not KJV: Mark Twain.

13. In the end, we will remember not the words of our enemies, but the silence of our friends.

13. Not KJV: Martin Luther King Jr.

14. The spirit indeed is willing, but the flesh is weak.

14. Matthew 26:41

15. When a thing is funny, search it carefully for a hidden truth.

15. Not KJV: George Bernard Shaw.

16. Seek, and ye shall find.

16. Matthew 7:7

17. Go, and do thou likewise.

17. Luke 10:37

18. God helps those who help themselves.

18. Not KJV: Benjamin Franklin, from *Poor Richard's Almanack* in 1757.

19. No one is useless in this world who lightens the burdens of another.

19. Not KJV: Charles Dickens.

20. Train up a fig tree in the way it should go, and when you are old sit under the shade of it.

20. Not KJV: Charles Dickens.

21. What goes around, comes around.

21. Not KJV: This is a folk saying, source unknown.

22. The weak can never forgive. Forgiveness is the attribute of the strong.

22. Not KJV: Mohandas Gandhi.

23. It is easy to despise what you cannot get. (The origin of the idiom, "sour grapes.")

23. Not KJV: Aesop's *Fables*, from the tale "The Fox and the Grapes." Fox cannot reach the grapes he desperately wants and says, "The grapes are sour anyway!" Hence, the moral of the story: "It is easy to despise what you cannot get." This is an example of how a phrase originated with the KJV (cf. Ezekiel 18:2), but the *idiom* got started later/elsewhere.

24. There is no new thing under the sun.

24. Ecclesiastes 1:9

25. Don't count your chickens before they hatch.

25. Not KJV: Aesop's *Fables*.

The average score was five wrong. Though not bad, it's still not a great score by high school grading standards: about a B minus. My unscientific test revealed what I had a hunch it would: that even those of us who are reasonably well-versed in the Bible don't always know for sure which popular phrases and sentences originated with the KJV and which originated elsewhere. That's good (unless you answered that #18 is in the "KJV"—a problematic misconception of a lot of Christians these days—but that's someone else's book!) because it means that the KJV has seeped into our language and into our lives.

We've inherited so many popular phrases from the great old Bible—phrases that have become cultural idioms—that it's impossible to name them all here. "Gather together ... from the four corners of the earth" (Isaiah 11:12). "Thou art ... found wanting" (Daniel 5:27). "Physician, heal thyself" (Luke 4:23). "Suffer fools gladly" (2 Corinthians 11:19). The KJV has influenced the English-speaking world more than any other book in history, completely out of proportion to what a simple book ought to be able to do.

This is because the KJV is not just a book; it is the most important translation of *the* book. The Word of God is the most critical and life-changing book in history. If you are reading *Verily, Verily*, chances are good that you believe the Bible to be more than just great literature, more than simply a cultural landmark; you turn to the Bible for instruction and inspiration.

But I'm making an additional point in the pages that follow: this particular translation—the KJV—has made a greater contribution to the literacy, culture, spirit, faith, and beauty of Western civilization than any other book in history. It marks a pinnacle of human understanding.

Until very recently, the KJV was the world's bestselling Bible in English. Sometime in the 1980s it was supplanted by the New International Version, which remains tops today. Still, there are more than one billion English-speakers in the world today, and there are at least two KJV Bibles in existence for each one of them.

The Gideons International alone has printed and distributed more than 1.5 billion Scriptures—both New Testaments and complete Bibles—since 1908. They gave away nearly 76 million last year alone! For their first eighty years, the Gideons distributed the KJV exclusively, but they have tended to favor the New King James Translation over the last two decades and make both translations available to their 280,000 members, in more than 10,000 local groups spread across the globe.[11]

If the Bible is a guidebook, or a manual, for living, then what does it mean that the most popular Bible over the centuries has been the KJV? It deserves to be rediscovered. To cast aside the KJV is to toss away a treasure chest of our culture and collective understanding. Today we are more secular, more global, and more multicultural than our forefathers and foremothers once were. All of these factors have caused us to look elsewhere. We no longer understand the KJV as representative of our culture. But the KJV still represents a significant slice of where we've come from, and the cultural heritage we've inherited from it has formed the world we live in, in ways that we may not even recognize.

SLOW DOWN AND READ

Playwright George Bernard Shaw said that the two books in every Irish Protestant home were *Pilgrim's Progress* by John Bunyan and the King James Bible. That was a century ago. More recently, the decline in biblical literacy has been well-documented. We don't know what our parents and especially our grand- and great-grand-parents knew of the Bible. But it's not just the Bible, or the King

---

11. When I asked the Gideons at their headquarters in Nashville for some firmer numbers I was told that they don't keep them, nor do they attempt to publicize them.

James Bible, that we no longer know; we also don't know heroic tales, myths, and epic poetry as earlier generations once did. I think the primary obstacle to knowing the Bible better is actually similar to why we don't read poetry much anymore. It was only a few decades ago that most daily newspapers regularly ran poems in their pages. Parents recited poems to their children as ways of reflecting and remembering lessons, virtues, and events. Kids memorized poems at school.

So it is with Scripture. It used to be a regular part of our lives, both private and public, and not simply because we all used to go to church more regularly. In a recent phone survey of 13,000 adults, 93 percent of Americans said that they have a Bible at home.[12] In colonial America, this percentage would have been 99.5 percent. A Bible was very often the only book to be found in a home, and it was in *every* home. Also in that survey, 75 percent of those with a Bible responded that they've read at least one passage from it in the last year. In another recent survey, conducted by Gallup, the number of those who said that they read their Bible "occasionally" was 59 percent, and this compared to 73 percent in the 1980s.[13]

One obstacle to reading and hearing the Bible today is, as it is for poetry, the *slowness* that it requires. Our time and attention is splintered in ways that Benjamin Franklin never could have imagined possible. As a result, few of us practice the discipline of reading slowly, and the KJV demands the slowest, most careful reading of any translation. Along with classic poetry and certain types of

---

12. This survey was conducted in 2008, commissioned by the Catholic Biblical Federation. Slightly more Protestants than Catholics reported having read the Bible in the last year, but the difference was statistically negligible.
13. Alec Gallup and Wendy W. Simmons, "Six in Ten Americans Read the Bible at Least Occasionally," The Gallup Organization, gallup.com/poll/2416/six-ten-americans-read-bible-least-occasionally.aspx (October 20, 2000).

music, appreciating the language of the KJV has almost become a lost art.

We've seen the advent of the slow-food movement (in 1989), and more recently, the slow-living movement, each of which are simply ancient wisdom made new. Slowness is praised throughout the Bible. Moses tells God that he is "slow of speech, and of a slow tongue" (Exodus 4:10), and then Moses learns that this is just fine; he's fully qualified for the job. God is praised for being "slow to anger"—over and over again, from Nehemiah to Psalms to Proverbs to the Prophets. Proverbs 14:29 says, "He that is slow to wrath is of great understanding." And then there is that verse my father would always quote to my brother and me: "Let every man be swift to hear, slow to speak, slow to wrath" (James 1:19). For a whole host of reasons that we'll explore in the coming chapters, we will see the beauty and wealth of the KJV—if we can learn to slow down.

THE FLOW OF STARTLING, ANCIENT WORDS

The KJV translators weren't interested in creating smooth, easy phrasings. Have you ever noticed that some of the most memorable radio voices aren't smooth? A couple of the most frequent on National Public Radio even have lisps and distinct regional accents. Others have quirky cadences and pronunciations—so that I know who is talking the moment that I hear their voice come over the airwaves. They are like celery to my ears! I seem to hear what *they* are saying better than what the smoother and easily digestible voices of other radio personalities are saying.

Similarly, the KJV translators worked to create an English version that was not entirely familiar or easy. Even as they turned unfamiliar languages (Hebrew and Greek) into the vernacular, they didn't always use everyday English. Some of the language would be unfamiliar. They did this because they believed that Scripture isn't always supposed to be easy; it's supposed to be challenging and even unusual. (See the Appendix for *A Quick Guide to Archaic Words and Phrases*, which includes common seventeenth century English words that are uncommon, today, but also some words that weren't even common when they were used in the KJV in 1611.) That's some of why the KJV sparks the imagination with a bit of strangeness. Compared to our language today, it has spit and stench, ghost and spirit, and isn't afraid to be earthy, honest, and — sometimes — downright odd.

Compare these two examples from the beauty of the KJV — "probably the most beautiful piece of writing in any language," according to H. L. Mencken. I've put the KJV and the recent, Good News Bible, side-by-side:

How forcible are right words!	*Honest words are convincing.*
—Job 6:25, KJV	—Job 6:25, GNB
For in much wisdom is much grief: and he that increaseth knowledge increaseth sorrow.	*The wiser you are, the more worries you have; the more you know the more it hurts.*
—Ecclesiastes 1:18, KJV	—Ecclesiastes 1:18, GNB

For one raised on the KJV, its language has a distinct pedagogical advantage: it's easier to remember. I've always found it easier to memorize Bible verses in the KJV, but perhaps that's because I got it in Sunday school. A kid today might have an easier time remembering "the more you know the more it hurts" (GNB) than she would, "he that increaseth knowledge increaseth sorrow" (KJV).

Still, there's a way in which we know "Fourscore and seven years ago ..." not just because our middle school teachers drilled it into our heads, but because it *sounds* biblical; Abraham Lincoln was, in fact, deliberately speaking in the deep resonances and cadences of the KJV.

Similarly, I find it easier to memorize and recall Philippians 4:13 in the KJV: "I can do all things through Christ which strengtheneth me," as opposed to "I can do everything through him who gives me strength" (NIV). To an ear trained to hear the music of the King's English, the first sounds like St. Paul to me. The second sounds like anything else.

Imagine how carefully you listen to someone speaking in halting English. I enjoy talking with cab drivers when I'm on a ride in Manhattan; I find most of them fascinating, and it's usually interesting to hear how they came to be in New York, to drive a cab, and so on. On one occasion, I discovered that my driver was from Bengal, the region of India that the great poet Rabindranath Tagore hailed from. "I love the writings of Tagore," I said to him.

And he lit up. "Really? ... You?" he said, flabbergasted that anyone in his new home would even know the name of India's most famous twentieth-century poet, the writer that the Bengalis call "the Shakespeare of India."

"Yes," I said. "You must have read him in school, yes?"

"Yes, yes, yes!" he said, still beaming, looking at me in the rearview mirror so often that I began to worry about what was in front of us.

"Do you miss your homeland?" I asked him.

And he responded in that way that people sometimes do when

they are speaking their second or third language. He said, "I ...
need, also ... home. I miss ... the places ... and my mother." I have
no doubt that I *heard* him more clearly than I would have if we were
both talking rapid, familiar shared language.

When Dr. Samuel Johnson was creating his famous English-
language *Dictionary* (1755), he explained in the preface his own
approach to archaic, or "obsolete," words: "Obsolete words are
admitted, when they are found in authors not obsolete, or when
they have any force or beauty that may deserve revival."[14] This is
precisely why the strange-sounding words in the KJV can not only
revive our language but draw people toward it. Easy understanding
is sometimes good, but at other times the unusual can help us to
see things more clearly.

As I've come to appreciate, some archaic words also have
broader meanings than first imagined. The vocative O, for instance,
offers some of the most beautiful moments in the KJV, such as
"Incline thine ear, O LORD, and hear" (Isaiah 37:17). And the inter-
jection *oh*, carries the involuntariness and surprise of the Yiddish
oy, including the sighing resignation. Can't you just hear Absalom's
oy in this verse: "Oh that I were made judge in the land" (2 Samuel
15:4)? Also, the use of older grammatical structures can mark the
best translations of classic texts. In these ways, the KJV Psalms are
simply gorgeous: "Cast me not away from thy presence; and take not
thy holy spirit from me" (51:11). We should treasure the old.

Richard Francis Burton did—when he translated *The Arabian
Nights* from Arabic into English in 1885. Rabindranath Tagore did,
thirty years later, when he set out to translate his own work from
its original Bengali into English. Tagore's *Gitanjali*, which brought

---

14. Samuel Johnson, *A Dictionary of the English Language: An Anthology*, David Crystal, ed.
(New York: Penguin, 2006), 27.

him a Nobel Prize in 1913, at times reads as if phrases were lifted directly from the KJV. "Here is thy footstool," one verse begins. Another begins, "If thou speakest not ..." and "Thou hast made me endless," begins another. Neither Burton nor Tagore strove for what we might call a "modern" or "contemporary" idiom; instead, they deliberately retained what was older, and therefore alluring, about the original. Both of these became quick bestsellers in their first English translations precisely because they used language that was more, not less, florid and fantastic. They created a *mood*. Our newer translations today certainly *communicate* the text more clearly, but they don't evoke as much of what it might *feel* like today to overhear Moses, David, Mary, Jesus, or Paul, speaking in Hebrew, Aramaic, or Koine Greek.

Another aspect of this mood in the KJV goes beyond idiom and language and enters into the arena of setting and scene. This is why great writers like Toni Morrison have fondly remembered the KJV being read in their family homes—precisely because the language, mood, and scenery were distinct from the world outside. If you prefer to imagine Jesus talking with a crowd outside one of today's shopping malls or with use of PowerPoint in a lecture hall, then the most contemporary English translations are your thing. But if you want to experience more of what it might have been like to be standing by the Sea of Galilee or in the Temple in Jerusalem, I believe that the older the English the better.

A LITTLE BIT OF HISTORY

I've met plenty of smart people who, upon learning that I'm writing a book about the KJV, have asked, "Why is it called that—was there a King James who sat down and translated it?" I've also talked with people who believe that the Christian Scriptures originated in the English language — that Jesus actually spoke English. Clearly, a short history lesson is in order. The story of the creation of the KJV is the story of a struggle, a dream, a nightmare for some, attempts at reconciliation, countless failures, and the creation of a massive, beautiful, spiritual work of art.

This isn't a story about men in lace frills, gowns, and high-heeled shoes translating a new English Bible — well, okay, that sort of thing *will* definitely play a part! But the story is much more: it is about the enduring influence of that Bible, created by men in high heels so long ago. Translating the Bible into common English, finally displacing the millennium-old Latin, was neither simple nor without conflict. We'll meet men who were tortured and executed for presuming to do such a thing. We'll meet the experts who were called together on the KJV translation committees in 1604. And we'll also see that the language of the KJV played a role in the rising predominance of English — rather than Latin — as the world's lingua franca.

What sorts of errors (many of them downright hysterical) crept into the translation and copying and recopying of the KJV? Many of these form the backbone of the humor in the KJV — and we'll explore that in chapter 4, "Lo, the Humor!" In chapter 5, we will explore why the KJV continues to be so popular in some parts of the world. There are those within Christianity who proclaim, "If it isn't the KJV, it isn't the Bible!" Where did this idea originate, and how does it persist? There are still thousands of churches in the U.S. that use only the KJV for study and worship. Which famous historical figures were indelibly stamped by their love of this translation, and how did it influence their work—and us? We'll get into that in chapter 6, "Great Lovers of this Book."

The KJV heritage in this country is rich. In the 1860s, soldiers on both sides of the Civil War carried only a few essential things in addition to their .58 caliber muskets. In their knapsacks and haversacks they would invariably have some writing materials, a toothbrush, tobacco, and a King James Bible. In fact, there are terrific stories of soldiers' lives being saved because bullets intended for them hit their Bibles instead. One of these was Private Walter G. Jones of the 8th New York Cavalry Company, whose pocket Bible shows where two holes have gone straight through (revealing a total of four clean holes when it is open to a passage), saving his life at the Battle of Cedar Creek in 1864.[15] These soldiers carried the KJV not because it was the preferred translation (for it was pretty much the only one available at that time) but because they believed that, by carrying it, they'd be in the presence of God. It wasn't long ago that the King James Bible was a powerful weapon against the onslaughts of life. It was as important, or more so, than daily food rations.

In the autobiographies, or "narrative lives," as they were often called, of freed African-American slaves, it was common to hear that a man or woman learned to read by reading the KJV. And it was often only the KJV that they learned to read, almost by the drive of desire or a miracle. In some cases, their reading was said to have begun, appropriately, with the first chapters of the Gospel of John:

> In the beginning was the Word, and the Word was with
> God, and the Word was God. The same was in the begin-
> ning with God. All things were made by him; and without

---

15. A daguerreotype of this Bible may be seen at the Library of Congress Digital Collection, currently at lcweb2.loc.gov/cgi-bin/query.

him was not any thing made that was made. In him was
life; and the life was the light of men. And the light shineth
in darkness; and the darkness comprehended it not.

1:1 – 5

Reading *this book* was the only reading that mattered.[16]

AN INVITATION TO IMMERSE THYSELF

The reach of the KJV has been far and wide—farther and wider
than any book in history—but understanding the KJV comes only
from reading it, hearing it, and absorbing it. *Verily, Verily* isn't an
academic exercise. My goal is to spark in you an interest in picking
up the KJV again. Spend time with it. Wander and explore. Enjoy.

I recently reread the entire 1611 KJV myself. I selected an edition that is without sectarian trappings of any kind—no footnotes,
commentaries, or devotional comments. I ignored my grandfather's
old Scofield Reference copy on the shelf, and my Thompson Chain
Reference from high school youth group. Instead, I picked an edition that was recently published by a university press, aimed at the
textbook market. The Old Testament accounts for 1,039 pages.
The Apocrypha (Grandpa would *not* have approved—but it was
included in the first KJV), 246, and the New Testament, 317. That's
1,602 pages all together; so I knew that if I read ten pages a day, I'd
finish in six months.

It was a journey I'll never forget—come with me and learn
what it was like. After all, the fewer Bibles I have to bury in my
backyard, the better.

---

16. See especially chapter 1 of Allen Dwight Callahan's *The Talking Book: African Americans
and the Bible* (New Haven, Conn.: Yale University Press, 2006).

SO MUCH AT STAKE

The word of the LORD was precious in those days.
1 SAMUEL 3:1

Precious. "In a costly or beautiful manner."
SHERMAN M. KUHN, MIDDLE ENGLISH DICTIONARY

I t is difficult to imagine how it was once possible for a nation to imprison and even execute its citizens for the crime of translating the Bible, but that's precisely what happened in England, one of the most civilized places on earth, for about 150 years.

A millennium before the era of Wycliffe and Tyndale, making translation a crime would have made about as much sense as passing a law against bareback squirrel riding or eating boats. Who would bother to legislate against something that no one wanted to, or perhaps could, do?

By the seventh century, however, the first spark of the idea to translate seems to have flared. According to the Venerable Bede (673–735), Caedmon, a monastery herdsman and the first English poet, paraphrased portions of the Old and New Testaments into Old English. Although modern scholarship now doubts whether many of those extant verses are Caedmon's originals, the "Caedmonian writings" consist of retellings of stories from Genesis, Exodus, and Daniel. Bede himself, just a generation after Caedmon, then translated portions of John's Gospel into Old English.

Two centuries later, King Alfred the Great (871–99), the most important medieval ruler of England, became a champion of vernacular learning. He was noted above all for his courageous and creative defeats of the invading hordes of Vikings. Detailed engravings and paintings, popular in every British elementary school textbook, show Alfred as a harp-playing minstrel in costume, spying in the camps of the Danes. There are also legends that he translated the Latin Bible into Old English. While that isn't exactly true — it was Alfred's scholars who did any such work — he *did* publicly lament the lack of Latin learning and the popular ignorance of both vernacular English and religion. Alfred translated several Latin texts, such as Pope Gregory I's *Pastoral Care*, into Old English. Much later, King Henry VIII (reign 1509–47) probably took his own inspiration to be a scholar-king from the legends of Alfred the Great. (More on that to come; Alfred found his way into the Catholic canon of saints — though Henry VIII wasn't so fortunate!)

How could an activity so seemingly innocent as translating the Bible into English be so threatening? It's not as if a theft or a murder or some other serious crime had been committed. This was simply translating Hebrew and Greek (or Latin) words and sentences into English equivalents. Where's the threat to national security? Why would this sort of activity be regarded as a way of undermining king and kingdom? The established order and status quo were in danger. By about 1380, translating Scripture into the vernacular became criminal, and attempting to translate the Bible became dangerous and clandestine work, like smuggling Bibles into Saudi

Arabia today. There was a lot at stake in such work — quite literally for some of the early translators and readers of the English Bible!

Speech has always been dangerous. Language carries ideas that can be infectious. Historically, words have demonstrated more power than swords to stir hearts and speak to souls. Some philosophers have even remarked that without speech and words human beings would be without souls.

In the Middle Ages, the words of God were believed to have been set in stone — complete and forever finished. They were not to be changed in any way. Never mind the issues that are now familiar to us about the reliability (or unreliability) of ancient or original texts, and the methods of transmission of those texts, and so on; for most people in the centuries before the KJV, messing with the particular words of God that they knew in the Latin Bible was like deciding to take a chisel and hammer to the Venus de Milo. Imagine a man who walks into the Louvre in Paris saying to himself, "I think I could take that unseemly angle off her nose with just a tap or two right about ... *there!*"

Every culture has been deadly serious about this sort of thing — not only the English and not only Christians. The privilege of faithfully repeating, copying, and rendering sacred words is of the utmost importance. The Vedas have a privileged place of honor in India. Throughout Indian history, traditionalist Hindus have proclaimed the Vedas' perfection, arguing that all knowledge is to be found in them, and that the way in which they are rendered in their original Sanskrit is infallible. Similarly, the Bhagavad Gita is most holy in Sanskrit — a language that hardly anyone but scholars can read. So it is with the words of Allah in the Qur'an. The original Arabic is believed to be directly revealed by God and not of human origin. The youngest of all of the world's major scriptures, the Qur'an existed only in Arabic until the early seventeenth century. Most Muslims today still believe that the Qur'an is the final revelation of God—but only in the original language.

In synagogues around the world, from the most liberal Reform to the most ultra-Orthodox, Jews even today only read the Torah in Hebrew. Torah scrolls are always handwritten—it can take a team of people a year or longer to complete one—and only *in* Hebrew. The ancient Greeks, prideful of their schools of philosophy and skills in rhetoric, coined the word *barbaroi*, from which comes our word *barbarians*, to describe those people who speak languages other than Greek. None of the world's major scriptures was translated before the first English translations of the Bible, with the exception of the Bible from its original Hebrew and Greek into Latin. Christians first presumed to do such a thing.

Soon after the death of Christ, Christians seemed anxious to translate the Bible into other languages. Christianity was the religion of many nations and many people, and hence all of the languages of the Mediterranean world. But thanks to the expanding reach of the Roman Empire, Latin became the single best way to unite people by about the year 400 CE.

DON'T MESS WITH JEROME

At the start of the fifth century, St. Jerome finished his magisterial work of translating the Bible into the vernacular Latin of the West. Jerome didn't finish the entire Bible by himself, but with the help of assistants and fellow translators he produced a Bible that most literate people in the Roman empire—and beyond—could read.

You don't have to be a nice guy to get things done, and Jerome was never known for his pleasant nature and kindly demeanor.

A Letter of St. Jerome

To Riparius, a presbyter of Aquitaine
[written in 404 CE, regarding the preaching of a certain clergyman]

Now that I have received a letter from you, if I do not answer it I shall be guilty of pride, and if I do I shall be guilty of rashness. For the matters concerning which you ask my opinion are such that they cannot either be spoken of or listened to without profanity. . . . You tell me that Vigilantius (whose very name Wakeful is a contradiction: he ought rather to be described as Sleepy) has again opened his fetid lips and is pouring forth a torrent of filthy venom . . .

I am surprised that the reverend bishop in whose diocese he is said to be a presbyter acquiesces in this his mad preaching, and that he does not rather with apostolic rod, nay with a rod of iron, shatter this useless vessel and deliver him for the destruction of the flesh that the spirit may be saved. . . .

The wretch's tongue should be cut out, or he should be put under treatment for insanity. As he does not know how to speak, he should learn to be silent.[17]

He also once wrote a letter to a Roman soldier named Exuperantius, urging him to come to Bethlehem, where Jerome himself was living, to become a monk. Exuperantius had asked Jerome for spiritual advice. According to another contemporary, Palladius, Exuperantius followed the suggestion, only to soon thereafter leave Jerusalem, "unable to endure Jerome's violence and ill-will."

---

17. This is known as Letter CIX in the Writings of St. Jerome, and the translation is from the online library: ccel.org.

Jerome may have had his comeuppance later in life, however. After a lifetime of intensely studying the Latin classics by such Roman writers as Seneca and Cicero, in order to create his Latin Bible, Jerome had a nightmare in which he stood before God on judgment day. "Who are you?" God asks him. "A Christian," Jerome replies. "You're a liar," God responds. "You're not a Christian at all. You're a Ciceronian!"

His baleful personality notwithstanding, Jerome was the greatest Christian scholar of his era and his legacy is the creation of the Latin Vulgate, the translation that became the Bible of Western Christendom for more than a thousand years. The venerability of the Latin—and the argument for the use of the Latin Bible for the next thousand years—was its univocality:

> It was the view of the Church that its singleness of voice and purpose could only be communicated if its entire corps of personnel worked from the same texts. And so, to promote unity of belief and uniformity of practice, the Church transmitted its official documents and pronouncements in a single language: Latin. Latin was the language of its doctrines; Latin was the language of its laws; and Latin was the language in which its sacred text, the Bible, was legitimately conveyed.[18]

Just as God was unchangeable, so was God's Word in Latin, according to the Church.

The original languages our Scriptures were written in were Hebrew (Old Testament) and Koine Greek (New Testament), but it was a Latin Bible that reigned supreme from about 400–1500 CE. We might say that the Vulgate was the first "authorized version."

---

18. Lori Anne Ferrell, *The Bible and the People* (New Haven, Conn.: Yale University Press, 2008), 33.

The earliest surviving, complete manuscript of the Vulgate is called the *Codex Amiatinus*. It dates from about the year 700 and was created in a monastery in the north of England, though it is currently housed in a lavish library in Florence, Italy. The *Codex Amiatinus* is huge. One of the innovations that came along with the Vulgate was to create for the first time a Christian Bible that was bound as a single volume. Before Jerome, and long after him too, the Bible was most often presented in many volumes. There were books of Gospels and Epistles and the Pentateuch, and so on. The *Codex Amiatinus*, weighing in at seventy-five pounds, has over 2,000 pages and is more than seven inches thick.

GAINING ACCESS TO THE HOLY OF HOLIES

The Vulgate wasn't a smash hit in the early fifth century when it was first made available. Jerome's Bible faced opposition similar to the first reception of the King James Bible more than a millennium later. By the beginning of the sixth century, however, this Latin Bible was considered the unalterable Word of God. And for the next near-millennium, the words of the Bible — as well as Bibles themselves — were basically reserved for the few clergy who could study and expound them to others. The Bible was deemed too important for the uneducated to handle. Just as ordinary people were not welcome to handle the sacraments, so too, it was pretty much hands off the Holy Scriptures!

Because books were so valuable — material and labor costs made them prohibitively expensive to produce — they were quite literally *chained to shelves* in monasteries, cathedrals, and convents. There were no library cards for those outside the monastery or cathedral walls. No checkout privileges. No browsing the stacks.

Books weren't freely circulated or discussed, and yet they were believed by nearly everyone to be holy keys to the very meaning of life and the afterlife.

During the thousand-year rule of the Vulgate, there were fragmentary translations available in Anglo-Saxon (also called Old English), as I mentioned, by Caedmon, Bede, and Alfred the Great's scholars. Aelfric of Eynsham (in Oxfordshire), an abbot, translated large portions of the Bible into Anglo-Saxon as well. But the only copies of these vernaculars were hidden away in remote monastery libraries, too valuable to be released. For most of the Middle Ages, a layperson couldn't access a Bible, even assuming he or she could read Latin.

Most people in those days believed that vernacular literature was somehow vulgar. As Tyndale would later argue at the height of his clandestine translating activities: "Saint Jerome also translated the Bible into his mother tongue: why may not we also? They will say it cannot be translated into our tongue; it is so rude."[19]

Books held a variety of serious ideas — some of which were enjoyed much more by the ruling classes than by everyday people. The Bible, for instance, included ideas such as:

+ The "divine right of kings" — hereditary sovereigns are ultimately accountable only to God.
+ The divine obligation of paying taxes. As Jesus said, "Render therefore unto Caesar the things which are Caesar's; and unto God the things that are God's" (Matthew 22:21).

In England as elsewhere, royalty and rulers enjoyed the power, and the resulting social order, these principles "mandated" — and it

19. David Daniell, *Tyndale's New Testament* (New Haven, Conn.: Yale University Press, 1989), xiv.

didn't hurt their grip on power that the people couldn't check the text for themselves.

During the Middle Ages, literacy was rare outside the privileged classes, so the Vulgate, even when available, was largely unread. Latin was rarely spoken, either. By about 1300, sermons were preached in vernacular Middle English in England, even though the Bible was not available in the language. The Scripture read in church was hardly ever understood, even though the preaching based on it was, and this began to seem wrong to certain believers.

A REBEL PRIEST

In the late 1370s or early 1380s, the popular Yorkshire priest and Oxford theologian John Wycliffe began creating vernacular versions of Holy Scripture. By 1382, he was duplicating copies of his translations. In their first incarnations, these were quite stilted, taking the Vulgate's Latin and finding the most literal English equivalents for the words. What often resulted were passages nearly as incomprehensible as the Latin had been, but Wycliffe and his students continued to revise and refine their translations.

Because Wycliffe believed in the ultimate authority of Scripture and the importance of a direct personal experience of God, he considered it essential for every man and woman in England to have access to the Bible in their native tongue. The history books often portray Wycliffe as a man who wanted to start a new faith — the Protestant faith. That wasn't his intention, however, nor could it have been. There was no such thing as a Protestant. Wycliffe was a Catholic reformer.

In an address to the king and Parliament, the reformer Wycliffe eloquently lays out his reasons why the pope in Rome has no legal, spiritual, or moral right to claim sovereignty over the Church of England (and in the process, as we'll see, he also lays claim for much more) ...

A Complaint of John Wycliffe

Exhibited to the King and Parliament

[presented to the boy king, Richard II, October 1377]

The first article is this: That all persons, of what kin, private sects, or singular religion, made of sinful men, may freely, without any letting, or bodily pain, leave that private rule, or new religion, founded of sinful men, and stably hold the rule of Jesus Christ, taken and given by Christ to his apostles, and for more profit than any such new religion, founded of sinful men. . . . The rule of Jesus Christ . . . is most perfect . . . and each rule . . . made of sinful men, is less perfect.

Wycliffe wanted to remove the trappings of faith that had grown up surrounding the Scriptures, revealing some essentials in the Bible that were rarely noticed in his day. In his efforts to do so, he was said to be "the king's man" for the ways that he championed and defended the causes of the king of England against the supposed rights of the pope.

Wycliffe didn't have much faith in the leaders of the church, believing they had lost their way by pursuing lordship, wealth, and power, both material and spiritual. In fact, he often said things like this about the religious orders:

I suppose ... that some friars, whom God shall see fit to teach, will be converted, and devoutly embrace the religion of Christ in its primitive purity; and abandoning their perfidy, shall seek or obtain from Antichrist, and return of their own accord to the primeval religion of our Lord. And then, like Paul, they will build up the church.[20]

That "Antichrist," Wycliffe's sometime name for the pope, demonstrates why this English translator is often called a "forerunner of the Reformation." He took his reform farther than most and insisted on nothing less than a return to the words of the Bible. If those words proved to disavow certain aspects of Christendom, then so be it.

Wycliffe's opinions were well-known even before his translations of Scripture were widely distributed. In the Peasants' Revolt of 1381, when mobs of laborers marched to London to protest the exploitation of workers, they chanted phrases they'd heard from Wycliffe. He had become one of their heroes for his insistence that English is the language of the people and no other language should be used to keep peasants from knowing the truth about the Bible or anything else. With the Peasants' Revolt, serfdom began to fade in England—and Wycliffe wanted to remove the spiritual serfdom of a people who couldn't understand the Bible.

He died painfully from a stroke at the end of 1384—but he was fortunate. Instead of being tortured and executed for writing all these polemics against the pope, monasticism, and the Catholic interpretation of the Lord's Supper, he died of natural causes. By 1388, hand-copied translations of Wycliffe's translations were circulating throughout England, often illuminated and bound in beautiful volumes as gifts. Many of these Wycliffite Bibles are still extant. In fact, there are more Wycliffite Bibles remaining in private collections and libraries than any other book from that period—a

20. *Tracts and Treatises of John de Wycliffe, D.D. with Selections and Translations from his Manuscripts, and Latin Works.* Robert Vaughan, ed. (London: Blackburn and Pardon, 1845). Found online at oll.libertyfund.org.

testimony to the popular hold they must have had on the imaginations of the English people. Wycliffe's Bible, however, was quickly outlawed; after his death, his followers continued his work in an atmosphere of increasing danger.

POLITICS AND THEOLOGY MIX

Wycliffe's polemics were as political as they were theological, and he was actually condemned to death—after his death. In 1401, King Henry IV of England passed through Parliament a law called "Of the Burning of Heretics," stating that anyone possessing illegal books, such as translated Scriptures, would be burned at the stake. The purpose of Henry's law was to condemn the teachings of Wycliffe and his followers, who were by then known as Lollards. No one knows for certain the origin of that derogatory term, but it seems likely to have come from a popular Dutch word, *lollaerd*, which meant someone who mumbles or mutters. Lollards were belittled as the uneducated, know-nothing champions of vernacular learning.

By 1407, Thomas Arundel, the Archbishop of Canterbury under Henry IV, called a church-wide synod at Oxford and condemned the Lollard movement, making it illegal to preach or teach theology without official sanction. They couldn't have these lay preachers and teachers going about the countryside explaining the Bible in a language that the people understood! The "Arundel Constitutions," as they came to be known, included a renewal of the forbiddance for any person to translate the Bible. Arundel wrote: "We therefore decree and ordain that no man shall, hereafter, by his own authority, translate any text of the scripture into English, or any other tongue ..."

The primary issue was authority — on whose authority may Scripture be interpreted or translated? Because of Arundel and others like him, portions of Middle English Scripture were made illegal from then until the early sixteenth century. As Alister McGrath explains it:

> To its Latin- and French-speaking critics, English was a barbarous language, lacking any real grammatical structure, incapable of expressing the deep and nuanced truths of the Bible in particular, and the Christian faith in general. This complaint, which had been implicit in much fourteenth-century dismissal of English as a serious language of faith, became explicit in an important debate at Oxford in 1401. Richard Ullerston defended English against its critics valiantly, but ultimately in vain. The debate concluded that English was not an appropriate language for the translation of the Bible. It was but a small step from this literary judgment to the essentially political decision to ban English language altogether from every aspect of English church life. This decision, taken in 1407–9 by Thomas Arundel ... had special relevance for the issue of biblical translation.... English thus became the language of the religious underground. To write in English was tantamount to holding heretical views. Even as late as 1513, John Colet — then dean of St. Paul's Cathedral, London — was suspended from his position for translating the Lord's Prayer into English.[21]

A few years ago, *BBC History Magazine* interviewed ten prominent historians, asking them to name the "Ten Worst Britons" of

21. Alister McGrath, *In the Beginning: The Story of the King James Bible and How It Changed a Nation, a Language, and a Culture* (New York: Doubleday, 2001), 33.

the last ten centuries—and Thomas Arundel won the distinction of being the fifteenth century's leading vote-getter. In the history of English culture, he is seen as something of a killjoy—in a category with Jack the Ripper, who took the award for the nineteenth century![22]

Wycliffe's written attacks against Pope Urban VI also earned him special recognition at the Council of Constance in 1415, a few years after the Arundel Constitutions and thirty years after Wycliffe's death. The council publicly wished, with a sort of bizarre longing for the past, that they could have burned Wycliffe at the stake when they had the chance. The church declared him a heretic posthumously, going so far as to send soldiers to exhume Wycliffe's remains from their resting place in a remote Lutterworth churchyard, crush them, burn them to ashes, and throw them in the nearby River Swift.

Wycliffe was both an iconoclast and a heretic. He disobeyed pope and king with stubborn flair, which made him a heretic; but he also challenged the one and only Latin Bible, a foundation to both civil and religious authority, which made him an iconoclast. Nevertheless, when pope and king unite in denouncing someone as evil, attention is often drawn to that person's cause. In the decades following Wycliffe's death, the small fire of vernacular translation spread rapidly.

By 1509, Dutch priest and theologian Desiderius Erasmus, who was himself preparing a Greek New Testament, was publicly poking fun (in his book *In Praise of Folly*) at the clergy of Europe for their ineptitude at protecting a Latin text that they could hardly even read in Latin, let alone in the original languages. When the more famous Catholic reformer Martin Luther took up the same sort of

---

22. See news.bbc.co.uk/2/hi/uk_news/4560716.stm.

work in Germany more than a century after Wycliffe's death, eventually translating the Bible into German (in 1521), he was treading a well-worn path. Threatening the power of Christendom with vernacular Bibles was no longer new, and such projects were being undertaken by new leaders.

From the Desk of Bishop Cuthbert of London

to Sir Thomas More
[written on March 7, 1528]

Since of late, after the Church of God throughout Germany has been infested with heretics, there have been some sons of iniquity who are trying to introduce into this country of ours the old and accursed Wycliffite heresy and its foster-child the Lutheran heresy, by translating into our mother tongue some of the most subversive of their pamphlets, and printing them in great quantity. They are, indeed, striving with all their might to defile and infect this country with these pestilential doctrines, which are most repugnant to the truth of the Catholic faith. It is greatly to be feared, therefore, that Catholic faith may be greatly imperiled if good and learned men do not strenuously resist the wickedness of the aforesaid persons.[23]

ENTER THE COURAGEOUS (AND SOMEWHAT CRAZY) WILLIAM TYNDALE

It was in those 1520s that William Tyndale first began openly breaking English law by publishing his own translations of the Bible, the

---

23. C. H. Williams, *English Historical Documents 1485–1558* (New York: Oxford University Press, 1967), 828–29.

first in English to be largely based on the original languages. Like the Christians of the twentieth century who smuggled Bibles into the Soviet Union during the Cold War, Tyndale saw his as a holy work, a civil disobedience that obeyed the law of God. Tyndale often worked in the middle of the night, in vacated buildings, away from the watchful eye of the king's men, ready to flee when the authorities got close. He was willing to die but, like the apostle Paul, wanted to keep living while there was work to be done. On one occasion, just a year before his first complete New Testament was published, Tyndale and a helper even escaped by night in a covered boat on the Rhine River.[24]

Tyndale was a populist in the Wycliffe tradition, raised among Gloucester farmers. He once explained his desire to make an English Bible that would be "a book for the plough-boy." Up until his time, it had only been a book (in its legal, accepted forms) for kings and bishops. He was a man of the people who wanted to transfer power from kings to the commoners by giving everyone the words of God in their own language.

Revelation 1:5–6 became, for Tyndale, a prophecy come true:

> Unto him that ... made us kings and priests unto God
> his father, be glory, and dominion for ever more. Amen.
> (Tyndale's translation)[25]

Try to imagine how incendiary this was. Tyndale was revealing the words of Scripture to people who may have never heard them before and presenting them in the most revolutionary way he could. He believed that a democratic, egalitarian Bible could lead to the overthrow of the established religious and political order. That's

---

24. David Daniell, *Tyndale's Old Testament* (New Haven, Conn.: Yale University Press, 1992), x.
25. Daniell, *Tyndale's New Testament*, 370.

why it was called treason. Thomas More, the King's Lord Chancellor, denounced every form of these vernaculars and referred to "the malignity of this present time, with the inclination of people to erroneous opinions."[26] He was frightened.

Tyndale's translations began to circulate throughout England by the 1530s, having been clandestinely printed abroad. He had his first complete New Testament printed in Worms (modern Germany) in 1526; his first Pentateuch (the first five books of the Old Testament) in 1530, and then the New Testament again in Antwerp in 1534. The 1526 version was smuggled into England, arriving in the deep hull of a boat moving slowly across the English Channel under the darkness of night. But on that moonless night the authorities were at the port looking for illegal Bibles, and they were promptly seized. Most of those copies were burned by the agents of Henry VIII's government. A later 1534 edition escaped the seaport and made it onto horse-carts, spreading quickly into the countryside and into the hands of the English people. Despite the law against owning one, tens of thousands of Tyndale's Bible were owned by English readers by this time. A popular movement had become full-grown. Perhaps this was made easier by its small size: about four inches wide and five inches tall. You could easily slip a 1534 Tyndale into your pocket!

Civil authorities were outraged because the land was full of Bible-reading lawbreakers. Religious authorities — the clerical establishment — were incensed because the laity now had portable Bibles they could read. The Bible of the clergy had become the Bible of the people, and the people were now empowered to ask such questions as:

26. Quoted in Peter Ackroyd, *The Life of Thomas More* (New York: Doubleday, 1998), 300.

+ "What did Jesus mean when he said …"

This was too much of a challenge to established religious authority, even including the pope and king.

+ "Why have you been telling us _____, when the text seems to say otherwise?"

A variety of religious ideas came under scrutiny, ideas that had grown up by tradition rather than by biblical teaching. For example:

+ The particular way the Liturgy of the Mass was celebrated
+ Formal sacraments apart from Baptism and the Lord's Supper
+ The veneration of saints
+ The leadership of a pope/bishop in Rome

Readers of Tyndale's Bible had trouble finding these practices or doctrines in the text. Soon other questions followed. Tyndale had translated "bishop" as "overseer" and replaced "church" with "congregation." This last one riled the pope in particular. Like Erasmus before him, Tyndale rendered the Greek work *ecclesia* to mean not a "church" but a "congregation." That one small word had an enormous impact. Matthew 16:18 changed from "You are Peter, and on this rock I will build my church" to "You are Peter, and on this rock I will build my congregation." Such translation choices undermined the longstanding institutional power from the central church (both in England and in Rome), instead empowering local believers.

Before vernacular Bibles, divine law — that is, God's will — was almost entirely encapsulated in the words of canon law, articulated exclusively by the church — the pope and his Roman curia (advisors, administrators, government). With vernacular Scripture, the intentions of God became housed in the words of the Bible itself, ready to be read by anyone and everyone. This was a dramatic shift of power — from curia to book. For Tyndale, the people in the pews were the *ecclesia*. Completing the power shift, he also changed "penance" to "repentance" and "confession" to "knowledge," shaking up the linguistic foundation of two of the seven holy Sacraments of the Church. His coup de grace was translating "priests" as "elders," empowering local churches to choose their own local leadership.

Unlike Wycliffe, Tyndale didn't escape a heretic's death. Heretics were being rounded up all over England. The authorities raided houses to search for vernacular books; possessing them was like possessing materials for building a bomb. Heretics were often humiliated before being imprisoned in the Tower of London or executed. In one typical instance, "condemned heretics were forced to ride, facing the horses' tails, with various of their texts pinned to their clothing.... During the journey from the Tower to Cheapside Cross, the citizens obliged by pelting them with rotten fruit and dung."[27]

Tyndale wouldn't escape death even by escaping England. Lord Chancellor Thomas More (quite poetically) characterized him as a "drowsy drudge drinking deep in the devil's dregs,"[28] and Tyndale was hunted down. Betrayed by English agents in Antwerp who were loyal to king and pope, Tyndale was strangled first, then burned at the stake on October 6, 1536. He quickly became a martyr of the Protestant cause. His followers compared him to the Hebrew prophets and to Moses, as one who toiled in the wilderness and died for a holy cause — without ever seeing his work come to fruition.

---

27. Ackroyd, *The Life of Thomas More*, 301.
28. Peter J. Thuesen, *In Discordance with the Scriptures: American Protestant Battles over Translating the Bible* (New York: Oxford University Press, 1999), 23.

THE TALE OF
TWO KINGS

*And after this Joseph of Arimathæa,
being a disciple of Jesus, but secretly . . .*

JOHN 19:38

The story of the King James Bible begins with the story of that most infamous of English kings, Henry VIII. King Henry is often identified as the only cause for England's split from the Roman Catholic Church and the creation of the Church of England, which happened two generations before the KJV was created. In actuality, the English had long felt that their island was the true center of the true church.

ANCIENT BRITISH CHRISTIANITY?

In the 1500s, schoolchildren in England were taught that the origins of their nation could be traced to the days of Horace and Cicero, when the ancient Romans invaded England before there ever was a first bishop of Rome. According to popular tradition, "Great Britain" takes its name from Brutus of Troy, the legendary figure reputed to be the first king of the Britons in 1100 BCE. According to this legend, which is impossible to verify, young Brutus accidentally kills his father with an arrow and is banished from his birthplace in Italy, where the family settled after his father returned from the Trojan Wars. After wandering through Gaul (the part of France that faces England), Brutus eventually crosses the English Channel and comes to settle in the land that has become known as *Britain*. He brings others to join him, starts a family, and the entire population of Britain ultimately descends from the man from Troy.

Brutus would have reigned in England at nearly the same time Eli served as a high priest in Israel. One legend has it that Brutus's genealogy traces back as far as Ham, one of the sons of Noah.

Poet William Blake also explored myths of England's special relationship with biblical characters. In the eighteenth century Blake wrote of the ancient druids as if they were the same people as the biblical patriarchs, and he wrote these famous lines, speculating that Joseph of Arimathea and the child Jesus may have actually come to England:

> And did those feet in ancient time
> Walk upon England's mountains green:
> And was the holy Lamb of God,
> On England's pleasant pastures seen![29]

According to this myth, Joseph of Arimathea—the wealthy businessman the Gospels say donated his own tomb for the burial of Jesus and who was thought to be the cousin of Mary—may have actually come to the shores of England with a very special companion. The Bible says nothing about the life of Jesus from age twelve until

---

29. William Blake, *Milton: A Poem*, copy B, Plate 2 (Princeton, N.J.: Princeton University Press, 1993 [orig. 1808]), 94.

about age thirty, and very little about his preadolescence. This legend (debunked by every scholar who hasn't been hired by Dan Brown's publicity firm) has it that Joseph was a merchant of metals used in construction, and tin was minted in Cornwall, England, in those days, so Joseph traveled there on business trips. On one such trip, Joseph of Arimathea is said to have brought the young Jesus with him from ancient Galilee—and the teenage Jesus walked around England!

Such cultural myths fed the notion that ancient England, more than Italy, had a valid claim to be the keeper and sustainer of classical learning, culture, and religion. The Germans didn't export Luther's Bible to the wider world, as the English did with their King James Bible. There's no famous Italian Bible, even though a vernacular version appeared before the beginning of the sixteenth century. It was the English who felt a sense of mission to spread their Bible, their culture, and their language throughout the world—they felt destined to do so.

Regardless of whether these English legends were true—and there were many more besides the ones just mentioned—they lit a fire of independent pride in all those English men and women who resented being forced to look to Rome for spiritual guidance. And the Rome they looked to was increasingly torn by scandal and schism. Christians in England felt a growing conviction that the office of the papacy had less and less relevance to their everyday lives. The human desire to know God more deeply began to look for answers in new places.

NOW ... KING HENRY VIII

In some ways, King Henry VIII—who we usually associate with abusive power, womanizing, and arrogance—gets a bad rap. He began his adult life an earnest Christian. He genuinely loved the Bible and championed its accessibility. Rarely do we hear about the many ways that Henry VIII used his royal position to promote the cause of the faith and the reading of the Bible.

In 1535, as Tyndale's European-printed and smuggled New Testaments were making their way into the kitchen cupboards of the English countryside, Henry VIII sponsored a portable edition of the Vulgate (excluding some of the duller books of the Old Testament), and even wrote a preface for it. He involved himself in various details, including selecting the typeface used in the printing, writing, "Although our [this is the royal *our*] eyes are still, by the grace of God, sharp enough, because they may, as is usual with advancing age, lose their strength, we have adopted a printing type which is, in our opinion, more suitable and easier to read."[30] This was a guy who enjoyed the details.

Within a year after Tyndale's death (1536), Henry VIII had begun to see a clear political need for an English Bible. He revered the Vulgate but came to believe that he could bring order to all of the vernacular fervor in his country.

He had other motivations too. It started to become clear to Henry that the Church of England was on a course of separating from the Church of Rome. And if England were to become independent, it made sense for England to have Holy Writ in the everyday English of the time. Loyalty to king — rather than to pope — became the new spiritual literacy.

Henry's motivations for this separation weren't all pure, however. He was a bit of a scoundrel who carried on several romantic affairs during his marriage to Catherine of Aragon, his first wife,

---

30. This little known story is told, and Henry VIII's preface quoted extensively, in Arthur Freeman, "To Guard His Words," *Times Literary Supplement* (December 14, 2007), 13–4.

and he soon was campaigning to have Pope Clement VII annul his marriage. Catherine, the widow of Henry's dead brother, Arthur, the Prince of Wales, had married Henry in 1509. They were married for a total of twenty-four years, and the first decade, at least, seems to have been a happy one. Still, all of Catherine's children died in infancy except for one girl, Mary, later to become the Catholic Queen who has come down in history as "Bloody Mary" for the number of Protestants she had executed.

So, after about sixteen years of marriage, Henry decided that having a male heir was more important than his marriage to Catherine. He wanted security for England, and this would come best through an orderly succession of power, from father to son. The previous centuries had seen disastrous wars of succession in England, and Henry wanted to avoid that at all costs.

After many difficult pregnancies, Catherine's doctors agreed that her body could not take another. It was then that Henry became infatuated with another woman, Anne Boleyn, one of Catherine's own maids of honor. Henry had already had an affair with Anne's sister, Mary. By 1527, Anne Boleyn acquiesced to the king's advances, and they became secretly committed to one another.

Anne relished her powerful new role as the king's mistress, but she was eager to play the role of queen as well and to enjoy the luxury and privilege that accompanied it. She was exacting and demanding of Henry in both public and private, becoming furious, for instance, when she learned that Henry was continuing to send his shirts to Catherine for mending.[31] But Anne was also clever, involved in religious matters, and even the daughter of a father (Thomas) who was himself a Protestant reformer.

---

31. Alison Weir, *The Six Wives of Henry VIII* (New York: Ballantine Books, 1993), 212.

During his relationship with Anne, Henry—a genuine student of the Scriptures—uncovered a verse in the Old Testament that he believed stated the truth about his marriage to Catherine: "If a man shall take his brother's wife, it is an unclean thing: he hath uncovered his brother's nakedness; they shall be childless" (Leviticus 20:21).

Henry took it as a sign from heaven, although it was a reinterpretation of history, to be sure. Catherine and Henry's brother, Arthur, had been married for less than five months before Arthur died. According to Catherine, that marriage had never been consummated. But Henry saw the verse as a way to legitimize ending his relationship with Catherine, and he believed that the Bible held a true prophecy for his life. Suddenly, in Henry's mind, Catherine had lied to him all of those years.

It was on these grounds that Henry sought an annulment. At the same time, he began to publish remarks to the churches acknowledging the growing importance of translating the Bible into English—and soon. He declared his intent to have this done in a formal, orderly way at the appropriate time.

BUILDING THE CASE FOR A DIVORCE

Henry knew that both the Old and New Testaments supported what was called the "divine right of kings." For instance, 1 Peter read:

> Submit yourselves to every ordinance of man for the Lord's sake: whether it be to the king, as supreme; Or unto governors, as unto them that are sent by him for the punishment of evildoers, and for the praise of them that do well. For so is the will of God, that with well doing ye

> *may put to silence the ignorance of foolish men: As free,*
> *and not using your liberty for a cloak of maliciousness,*
> *but as the servants of God. Honor all men. Love the*
> *brotherhood. Fear God. Honor the king.*
>
> 2:13–17

Kings were higher than the clergy. Kings were not *secular* rulers in the worldview of Christendom. Perhaps it was time for the king of England formally to become the spiritual leader of England as well.

Henry shrewdly played on his people's feelings of nationalism. Even as he was petitioning the pope to annul his marriage, he was preparing to sidestep the pope entirely, if need be. In 1530, Henry sent Thomas Cranmer to Rome, circumventing the appropriate channels because his cardinal, Thomas Wolsey, objected. The word *annul* literally means "to declare invalid or void." The *Catechism of the Catholic Church* puts it like this in paragraph 1629:

> For this reason (or for other reasons that render the marriage null and void) the Church, after an examination of the situa-tion by the competent ecclesiastical tribunal, can declare the nullity of a marriage, i.e., that the marriage never existed. In this case the contracting parties are free to marry, provided the natural obligations of a previous union are discharged.

Pope Clement VII refused to annul Henry's marriage, and Henry, inspired by the ideas of people like Tyndale (whom Henry had already spent a great deal of energy condemning), began to think, *Shouldn't the words of Scripture take precedence over the words of the pope?*

Henry's close advisor, Thomas Cromwell, urged him to have Parliament declare him the supreme head of the Church of England.

By February 1531, it was done, and by August, Henry had banished Catherine from her rooms in the palace and given them to Anne.

Henry VIII and Anne Boleyn married in January 1533. Anne was already pregnant at the time. (That daughter, Elizabeth, would later become Queen Elizabeth I of England.) Only a few years later, however, Anne also fell out of favor. She had miscarried at least twice and failed to give Henry the son that he coveted. The sharp-witted, stylish, opinionated "other woman" quickly became the victim of trumped-up accusations of adultery and even incest — charges that most historians, including contemporaries of Henry VIII, have rejected. She was taken to the Tower of London and executed on May 19, 1536.

THE FIRST *AUTHORIZED* ENGLISH BIBLES

If the pope had remained the supreme head of the English Church, the Vulgate would have remained the only Scripture for the people of England much later than it did. The creation of vernacular Bibles was prompted by the belief that God was at work in England and that it was the English themselves who were in the best position to understand — and carry out — that work. Henry VIII was now ready and willing to acknowledge that his people deserved access to what was rightfully theirs: an English Bible.

Under Henry's general sanctioning of English Bible translation, several versions appeared, a good eighty years before the KJV. First, was the Coverdale Bible in 1535, which Myles Coverdale translated and dedicated to the king. Although Coverdale reproduced much of what William Tyndale had translated illegally a decade earlier (they had, in fact, spent time in exile working together on the Continent), Coverdale also added his own brilliant linguistic skills to the task. It was published in Europe, not England, just as Tyndale's works had been. The Coverdale Bible was also produced in a useful format — only slightly larger than 8½ x 12½.

We have already seen the powerful phrasings of Tyndale, and we can see the same in the work of his friend. Most memorable of Coverdale's contributions comes from the poignant Psalm 23. It was he who first used the phrase "the valley of the shadow of death" in verse 4, which was then retained in the KJV.

In 1537, two years after the first Coverdale, Matthew's Bible was also sanctioned by Henry VIII. This version was named for Thomas Matthew — a pseudonym for Oxford scholar and editor John Rogers. This was a momentous shift in policy since Tyndale was burned at the stake: Henry VIII had begun allowing English translation generally.

Then came the second edition of the Coverdale Bible, published in 1539. This version — produced mostly in France, since English printers were unable to do such detailed work — created problems, since the Catholic Counter-Reformation was then in full swing. French authorities worked to prevent yet another Protestant Bible from being published and thousands of printed sheets were destroyed. Myles Coverdale himself, who went to France to oversee the presses, worried for his safety.

The name of the Coverdale second edition — the Great Bible — was due more to its immense size than to its prominence. It was intended for use on a church lectern and was far too large and expensive for personal use. Archbishop of Canterbury and soon-to-be editor of the Book of Common Prayer, Thomas Cranmer, wrote a special preface for the second printing, and in May 1540, Henry VIII issued a decree that the Great Bible was free from heresy and to be read in all of the churches in England. It was the first complete Bible to be personally commissioned and authorized by an English King. How times had changed in less than four years since Tyndale was burned at the stake—by Henry's men!

The reception of these vernacular Bibles was enthusiastic. One bishop went to great lengths to admonish his people to stop reading "inconsiderately and indiscriminately." He reported that the people were tending to "read especially and chiefly at the time of divine service ... yea in the time of the sermon."[32] An odd complaint, at least by today's standards!

Another historian writes of the joy that characterized these early days: "When the king had allowed the Bible to be read in the churches, immediately several poor men in Essex ... bought the New Testament, and on Sunday sat reading it in the lower end of the church; many would flock about to hear the reading."[33]

One of the earliest biographers of Thomas Cranmer recounted it this way:

> It was wonderful to see with what joy the book of God was received, not only among the learneder sort and those that were noted for lovers of the reformation, but generally all England over among all the vulgar and common people; with what greediness God's word was read, and what resort to places where the reading of it was. Everybody that could bought the book and busily read it; or got others to read it to them, if they could not themselves.[34]

---

32. Quoted in the classic work of Brooke Foss Westcott, *A General View of the History of the English Bible*, 3rd Edition (London: Macmillan & Co., 1905), 80.

33. Westcott, *A General View of the History of the English Bible*, 81.

34. Quoted in Benson Bobrick, *Wide as the Waters: The Story of the English Bible and the Revolution It Inspired* (New York: Simon & Schuster, 2001), 151–52.

This was simply too much for the Catholic Church of the mid-sixteenth century. In 1545, Pope Paul III — the pope who had first excommunicated King Henry VIII — called the Council of Trent in order to stabilize the church in the midst of what had become a continent-wide Protestant upheaval. One of their declarations over the course of the nearly two-decades-long council was to pronounce Jerome's Vulgate the *only* valid version of the Bible: "The same holy council ... ordains and declares that the old Latin Vulgate Edition, which, in use for so many hundred years, has been approved by the Church, be in public lectures, disputations, sermons and expositions held as authentic, and that no one dare or presume under any pretext whatsoever to reject it."[35]

The language of this decree goes so far as to state that only the Vulgate can communicate the Word of God in Scripture, and people should never be presumptuous enough to think they can interpret the Bible on their own: "Furthermore, to check unbridled spirits ... no one relying on his own judgment shall, in matters of faith and morals pertaining to the edification of Christian doctrine, distorting the Holy Scriptures in accordance with his own conceptions, presume to interpret them."

Scripture, and its interpretation, belonged only to "holy mother Church ... to judge of their true sense and interpretation," and, "those who act contrary to this shall be made known by the ordinaries and punished in accordance with the penalties prescribed by the law."

If someone like Martin Luther or Myles Coverdale had thought of visiting Rome on vacation in 1545, he would have been promptly

---

35. The following quotes are taken from the "Decree Concerning the Canonical Scriptures," Fourth Session Council of Trent, April 8, 1546. Currently available at csun .edu/~hcfll004/trent4.html.

arrested and treated to a nasty trial. In July 1555, when Henry VIII's Catholic daughter, Queen Mary I, ascended the throne of England, the Great Bible ceased to be printed, and John Rogers, one of the translators on whose work the Great Bible was partly based, became the first Protestant martyr of her reign. To be fair to the Catholics, though, this perspective of holding on tight to the Vulgate was held by the English kings and clergy until only a few years before.

Mary's reign, however, as well as her attempt to bring England back into the Roman Catholic fold were short lived. During her five-and-a half-years as queen, she proved to be increasingly unpopular among the people both for her persecutions of Protestants and her politically motivated marriage to a Spanish prince. When she died of natural causes in 1558, leaving no male heir, she was succeeded by her Protestant half-sister, Elizabeth.

There are two additional English Bibles that should be mentioned before the KJV — both completed during Elizabeth I's reign. The Geneva Bible of 1560, translated by English Protestants living in exile in Switzerland during the reign of Catholic Queen Mary I, was the first true study Bible, full of notes, tables, maps, concordances, and other tools for personal use. It introduced the important innovation of verse numbering, something that has become so common now that we can't imagine the Bible without it. The famous Puritan writer John Milton enthusiastically endorsed the Geneva Bible. This important translation has also been called "The Breeches Bible," because of the distinctive way that Genesis 3:7 was rendered: "Then the eyes of them both were opened, and they knew that they were naked, and they sewed fig tree leaves together, and made them selves breeches." (The KJV uses "aprons," and more recently the New Revised Standard Ver-

THE TALE OF TWO KINGS

sion, "loincloths.") The translators of the Geneva Bible made other interesting decisions; for instance, they used the following heading for the passage of Genesis 25 in which Esau loses his birthright: "Esau selleth his birthright for a mess of pottage."

The title page of the first edition of the Geneva Bible explains the approach taken: "The Bible, that is, the Holy Scriptures contained in the Old and New Testaments, translated according to the Hebrew and Greek, and conferred with the best translations in divers languages. With most profitable annotations upon all the hard places, and other things of great importance ..." *All the hard places* — this was the first time that translators and Bible scholars had tried to explain the complicated verses to laypeople. But in the same translators' preface, their very Protestant approach was made plain when they explained the need for this new Bible to combat the "horrible backsliding and falling away from Christ to Antichrist, from light to darkness, from the living God to dumb and dead idols." They were identifying the pope with the Antichrist. The Geneva Bible went on to identify the "Whore of Babylon" in Revelation 17:4 with "the Antichrist, that is, the Pope."[36] Vernacular Bibles had become fully identified as a Protestant innovation; they were a dividing line.

Then came the Bishops' Bible of 1568, created by a sector of the Church of England dissatisfied with the Calvinism that dominated the Geneva Bible. The first editions carried a portrait of Queen Elizabeth I on their title pages. The KJV borrows some phrases and passages from the Bishops' Bible. In fact, first among the principles of translation that guided the KJV was this one: "The ordinary Bible read in the Church, commonly called the Bishops' Bible, to

---

36. Peter J. Thuesen, *In Discordance with the Scriptures: American Protestant Battles over Translating the Bible* (New York: Oxford University Press, 1999), 26.

be followed, and as little altered as the Truth of the original will permit."

Although the Bishops' Bible became the official Bible of the Church of England, to replace the Great Bible, it was not admired as the Geneva Bible was. The Bishops' Bible was overblown, excessively verbose, even haughty at times in its word choices. For example, it is sometimes called "The Treacle Bible" because of the distinctive way that the first portion of Jeremiah 8:22 was rendered: "Is there not treacle at Gilead?" The KJV used the memorable alternative made famous by Dr. Martin Luther King Jr. in various speeches, including one to striking workers in Memphis in the year of his death: "Is there no balm in Gilead?"

All of these Bibles were circulating throughout the English-speaking world at the time that King James I ascended the throne of England in 1603.

KING JAMES I

Due to its Puritan adherents, the Geneva Bible was the most common one in use by the time James I came to rule England, and he had more than a quibble with some of its extensive study notes.

The Protestant reformers who wrote them took every opportunity to elucidate passages in ways that detracted from certain established ideas like the "divine right of kings." The KJV version of Psalm 105:15 — "Touch not mine anointed, and do my prophets no harm" — doesn't differ from the versions of Tyndale or Coverdale and the Geneva Bible. But the Geneva Bible's notes added a slant. Its translators explained Psalm 105:15 by saying that "mine anointed" included only "those whom I have sanctified to be my people. Meaning, the old fathers, to whom God showed himself plainly, and who set forth his word." Every dedicated Christian could become *anointed*, not just a king or queen.

Or consider Daniel chapter 6, which tells the story of Daniel in the Lions' Den. Verse 22 reads in the KJV, "My God hath sent his angel, and hath shut the lions' mouths, that they have not hurt me: forasmuch as before him innocency was found in me; and also before thee, O king, have I done no hurt." But the note explaining this in the Geneva Bible contends that Daniel "disobeyed the King's wicked commandment in order to obey God, and so he did no injury to the king, who ought to command nothing by which God would be dishonoured." Such antimonarchical comments were intolerable to James.

James wanted to be sure that the rule of law was followed in England, and this included a preservation of what he believed to be the proper role of the sovereign. On religious matters, he tried to walk a middle road between the Protestant and Catholic conflicts, so he had no patience for those he believed to be religious fanatics who were only stirring up dissent and violence in his country.

Born and bred in Scotland — where John Calvin's Geneva reforms guided Protestant life — James, in fact, considered himself a Protestant, despite the fact that his mother, Mary Queen of Scots, had been a Catholic. But James was no Puritan. In the spirit of Queen Elizabeth I before him, James wanted to maintain the strength of the English throne against all who might challenge it — Protestant or Catholic. To James, the divine right of kings, and the unified peace it could provide England, was surely more important than splitting doctrinal hairs. It was for these reasons that he came to call the Geneva Bible the worst of all English translations.

King James longed for a vernacular, English-language Protestant Bible that would unite his English people without undermining his kingship. Within ten months of assuming the throne, James called for a new translation. The people of England, James believed, needed a Bible to *unite* them as Christians and as subjects of the king.

MASTERPIECE
BY COMMITTEE

The sacrifices of God are a broken spirit: a broken and a
  contrite heart,
  O God, thou wilt not despise.

PSALM 51:17

Contrite. Adjective.
"Bruised, contrite; worn or broken by rubbing."

DR. SAMUEL JOHNSON

I
t was in this very room," one of my hosts explained as we crossed
the threshold of the ornate Jerusalem Chamber, "that most of
the work of translating the King James Bible was done." I was
there for a simple book-launch party, a guest of the dean of Westminster, along with dozens of others. All night long I was imagining the conversations, arguments, quill pens, and yes, those lace
frills, that must have filled such a chamber from 1604 until the
great Bible went to press in early 1611.

In one corner of the room was the elegant and brilliant Lancelot
Andrewes, leader of the group working on Genesis through 2 Kings.

Did they lose a bit of steam as they passed 1 Samuel and moved into 2 Samuel and on through both Kings? I sure would have. I imagined them laboring into the night, feeling the importance of their work, candles flickering as they passed papers across long tables, scribbled notes and corrections to each other's work, and debated over the most appropriate renderings of difficult Hebrew and Greek phrases.

The Jerusalem Chamber was originally built in the 1300s. Not on the regular tours of Westminster Abbey, its name was most likely inspired by tapestries of the Holy Land that once hung on its cedar-paneled walls. The vaulted room became legendary long before any of King James's translators set foot inside. King Henry IV had died there in 1413, the result of a stroke suffered while he was praying in the Abbey church down the hall. Henry's attendants rushed him to the chamber because they knew a fire was roaring in its large fireplace.

"Where am I?" Henry is said to have asked. "The Jerusalem Chamber," he was told, which must have sounded eerie to a man only half-conscious and on the threshold of the hereafter — *particularly* to one about whom it had been prophesied that he would die in Jerusalem. Henry had much earlier usurped the throne from King Richard II but had pledged to make a pilgrimage to the Holy Land in order to atone for his sin. This story is told, among other places, in William Shakespeare's plays, *Richard II* and *Henry IV, Parts 1* and *2*.

The Jerusalem Chamber was the primary workspace used by King James's translation committees. It was chosen again by the organizers of the Revised Standard Version (New Testament released in 1881, and the whole Bible in 1885), men who wanted to communicate continuity with the past (more on this later). The chamber was also used by the committee working on the New English Bible, which was released in 1961.

THE MOOD OUTSIDE

It has been said that the KJV is the only masterpiece of the English language produced by committee. The likelihood that a loosely organized group of dozens of brilliant and opinionated scholars and clergy would translate, draft, revise, and polish the seminal text of modern Western English is staggeringly low—yet there is the King James Bible, a work of art with at least fifty artists.

There are several ways the translators could have failed.

First, the history of violence between Protestant and Roman Catholic Christians made collaboration hazardous. The rule of law in England had defended hangings, imprisonments, and banishments, depending on who happened to be sitting on the English throne at the time. Battles between Catholics and Protestants marred the century leading up to James I's reign, both nationally and internationally. Several decades before James took the throne, for example, Pope Sixtus V signed a treaty with Spain in which he pledged one million gold ducats (a king's ransom) to Spain's Philip II if he succeeded in conquering England and returning it to faithfulness to the Papal See.[37]

Within England, the KJV was started at the height of the Puritan influence over the Church of England. The reign of James I was seen by Puritans as a renaissance of Protestant possibilities. The Puritans, viewing themselves as distinct from the Church of England, believed that James would look kindly on their movement, but they

---

37. Alice Hogge, *God's Secret Agents: Queen Elizabeth's Forbidden Priests and the Hatching of the Gunpowder Plot* (New York: HarperCollins, 2005), 3–4.

were soon disappointed. The Puritans presented James with a petition of grievances and recommendations for reforms in the Church of England, which were discussed in January 1604 at what was called the Hampton Court Conference. At the end of three days, the King responded that he was little interested in the complaints of English Puritans, that the one thousand clergy who had signed the petition should be reminded to obey their bishops, and their bishops were to obey the king, who ultimately ruled the English Church. And, by the way, there were to be no more religious petitions!

The status quo was just fine for King James, thank you very much — yet it was a precarious balance between internal and external conflicts over politics and religion. Such a tenuous peace was unlikely ground for the pioneering editorial consensus that would become the King James Bible.

Even as James rejected the Puritans' petition, however, he did give them some little encouragement by agreeing with their call for a new translation of the Bible, for reasons we have already explored. The bishop of London, Richard Bancroft, who later became Archbishop of Canterbury, muttered against the idea of yet another English Bible: "If every man's humor might be followed, there would be no end of translating." For James, this was of little concern. The King knew that a new translation could replace the versions he didn't like, as well as create a lasting monument for the church with James as its head.

Bancroft would become the organizer of the king's project, which James summarized as: "I wish some special pains were taken for an uniform translation, which should be done by the best learned men in both Universities, then reviewed by the Bishops, presented to the Privy Council, lastly ratified by the Royal authority, to be read in the whole Church, and none other."

The hope was to create a Bible for the entire church that reached above Puritan and Catholic divisions. The translation committees would eventually respond by taking a step back and declaring how they intended to find a middle ground between the factions.

Remember that hubbub about the word *ecclesia* going back to Tyndale? In the KJV translators' statement of guiding principles, number three would become: "The Old Ecclesiastical Words to be kept, viz. the Word Church not to be translated Congregation &c." New texts had become available in recent years; the understanding of Greek and Hebrew had deepened in the universities; and the English language itself had evolved from the Middle English of Chaucer and Wycliffe closer to what we know as English today. So the KJV was created out of a tsunami of opinion that the church needed reforming. The king's new Bible would try to be for everyone, without discrimination.

Mutual distrust continued, however, despite the goals of King James. English fear of Catholicism—as an "outside" and insidious influence—was given tangible evidence late the following year, in the 1605 Gunpowder Plot. One of the most notorious attempts at religious terrorism ever, right up there with Samson collapsing the temple of the Philistines, the Gunpowder Plot was an attempt to assassinate King James I and his family, blow up both Houses of Parliament at Westminster, and incite violence throughout the country in the days that followed. An explosives expert and Catholic revolutionary named Guy Fawkes was captured before he could carry out the deed. He was later tortured in the Tower of London and executed.

The second great obstacle facing the translation committee was the bubonic plague, known as the Black Death. The year before the

KJV committee began their work was one of the worst years for the city of London. More than a thousand people died each week in London in 1603 alone, when city officials blamed cats and dogs for the spreading of the contagion. Children were paid a small reward for each dead animal, a practice that allowed the true carriers of the disease — rats infested with diseased fleas — to flourish. As fear and death spread across the Great City, it seemed unlikely that the king's translation project would have much success. The Hampton Court Conference had originally been scheduled for November of 1603 but was delayed until January of 1604 because of the plague. But once it started, perhaps long days and nights of secluded work in the Jerusalem Chamber helped keep those translators from contagion!

THE TRANSLATORS BEGIN TO GATHER

Despite these hindrances, an incredible assembly began to gather. The greatest minds of the day were brought together, among them scholars, teachers, bishops, and several terrific prose stylists. There were six committees in all, with several translators assigned to each one, and each committee was assigned to different portions of Scripture:

+ Genesis to 2 Kings

+ 1 Chronicles to Song of Solomon

+ Isaiah to Malachi

+ Matthew to Acts, and Revelation

+ The Epistles

+ The Apocrypha

They met in three cities, in Oxford at the university, in Cambridge at the university, and in Westminster in the Jerusalem Chamber. Fifteen guidelines were drawn up for the translators to guide their work, approved by the king. We've already mentioned some of them, and the reasons for some of the others will now be clearer to you. The first seven read as follows:

> The ordinary Bible read in the Church, commonly called the Bishops Bible, to be followed, and as little altered as the Truth of the original will permit.
>
> The names of the Prophets, and the Holy Writers, with the other Names of the Text, to be retained, as nigh as may be, accordingly as they were vulgarly used.
>
> The Old Ecclesiastical Words to be kept, viz. the Word Church not to be translated Congregation &c.
>
> When a Word hath divers Significations, that to be kept which hath been most commonly used by the most of the Ancient Fathers, being agreeable to the Propriety of the Place, and the Analogy of the Faith.
>
> The Division of the Chapters to be altered, either not at all, or as little as may be, if Necessity so require.
>
> No Marginal Notes at all to be affixed, but only for the explanation of the Hebrew or Greek Words, which cannot without some circumlocution, so briefly and fitly be expressed in the Text.
>
> Such Quotations of Places to be marginally set down as shall serve for the fit Reference of one Scripture to another.

Number 8 is fascinating. This principle set the KJV apart from the translations that had come before it. This is where we truly see how it became a masterpiece by committee!

Every particular Man of each Company, to take the
same Chapter or Chapters, and having translated or
amended them severally by himself, where he thinketh
good, all to meet together, confer what they have
done, and agree for their Parts what shall stand.

Numbers 9 through 12 then show even further how the committees challenged each other, and sought to be challenged by
other experts throughout the country:

As any one Company hath dispatched any one Book
in this Manner they shall send it to the rest, to be
considered of seriously and judiciously, for His Majesty
is very careful in this Point.

If any Company, upon the Review of the Book so sent, doubt
or differ upon any Place, to send them Word thereof; note
the Place, and withal send the Reasons, to which if they
consent not, the Difference to be compounded at the
general Meeting, which is to be of the chief Persons of
each Company, at the end of the Work.

When any Place of special Obscurity is doubted of, Letters
to be directed by Authority, to send to any Learned
Man in the Land, for his Judgement of such a Place.

Letters to be sent from every Bishop to the rest of his
Clergy, admonishing them of this Translation in
hand; and to move and charge as many skilful in the
Tongues; and having taken pains in that kind, to send
his particular Observations to the Company, either at
Westminster, Cambridge, or Oxford.

And then 13 through 15 simply round out some remaining
details.

> The Directors in each Company, to be the Deans of Westminster, and Chester for that Place; and the King's Professors in the Hebrew or Greek in either University.
>
> These translations to be used when they agree better with the Text than the Bishops Bible: Tyndale's, Matthew's, Coverdale's, Whitchurch's, Geneva.
>
> Besides the said Directors before mentioned, three or four of the most Ancient and Grave Divines, in either of the Universities, not employed in Translating, to be assigned by the vice-Chancellor, upon Conference with the rest of the Heads, to be Overseers of the Translations as well Hebrew as Greek, for the better observation of the 4th Rule above specified.

Overall, it is interesting how much of the committees' work was to be done through comparing texts in the various Bibles and taking what was best from all of them. In the preface to the first KJV, the translators said: "Truly, good Christian Reader, we never thought from the beginning that we should need to make a new translation, nor yet to make of a bad one a good one; but to make a good one better, or out of many good ones one principal good one."

COMING TO A WELL WITHOUT A BUCKET

In their 1611 preface, where they make a persuasive case for the necessity of a new English translation of the Bible, the translators begin by pointing back to Julius Caesar, thanking the old Roman Emperor for "correcting the Calendar, and order[ing] the year according to the course of the sun." They point out how courageous Caesar was to buck convention by doing so, and yet, "this was imputed to him for novelty, and arrogancy, and procured to him great obloquy."[38] Such historical analogies were intended to guard against those who would later try and tear down the translators' work.

Translation into the vernacular is necessary, they conclude, despite any possible objections. "But how shall men meditate in that which they cannot understand?" they plead. Even if a person reads and understands Hebrew, Greek, or Latin, that person must understand that the vast majority of Christian people cannot. Beautifully, the translators continue their case; it's easy to see how there were a few poets on the committees:

> Translation it is that openeth the window, to let in the light; that breaketh the shell, that we may eat the kernel; that putteth aside the curtain, that we may look into the most holy place; that removeth the cover of the well, that we may come by the water; even as Jacob rolled away the stone from the mouth of the well, by which means the flocks of Laban were watered. Indeed without translation into the vulgar tongue, the unlearned are but like children at Jacob's well (which was deep) without a bucket or something to draw with: or as that person mentioned by Isaiah, to whom when a sealed book was delivered with this motion, "Read this, I pray thee," he was fain to make this answer, "I cannot, for it is sealed."

PULLING TOGETHER THE MASTERPIECE

Translating the KJV took seven years. The various committees were formed with a mix of experts in Hebrew, Greek, and Aramaic,

---

38. All quotations from the King James Bible, its various books as well as the translators' preface, are taken from the edition of Robert Carroll and Stephen Prickett, mentioned above.

writers of distinction, and orators—the latter because, from the beginning, the KJV was intended to be read aloud in the churches. One of the intellectuals of that time wrote this account of how the translations were often fine-tuned:

> That part of the Bible was given to him who was most excellent in such a tongue (as the Apocrypha to Andrew Downes), and then they met together, and one read the translation, the rest holding in their hands some Bible, either of the learned tongues, or French, Spanish, Italian, etc. If they found any fault, they spoke up; if not, he read on.[39]

Most of these men were "divines," a term which can spark the imagination—but don't let yourself get too carried away. Divines are what clerics and theologians of the Church of England were once called. Lancelot Andrewes was a supreme example: this Bishop of Chichester, Ely, and then Winchester, assisted at the coronation of King James I. Respected in every hall of the kingdom, he was put in charge of the entire translation effort. For all of the divines, the name and vocation *did* come with a costume, and our translators were usually at work wearing long black gowns made of satin, adorned with linen ruffs protruding at the wrists and neck.

Except for the Puritans, who had long ago eschewed fancy clerical dress. Still, they brought a fierce passion for discovering the meaning of Scripture to the table. James had insisted that his Bible bring all of the factions of England together, and for that reason, the more moderate among the Puritans were included. A diehard Puritan would never have accepted such a commission from the

---

39. From the Table Talk of John Selden (1584–1654), quoted in Alister McGrath, *In the Beginning*, 33.

king (separatist that he was), which is why we only see moderates among the translators—and they accounted for half of the total. One academic has explained the contrast between the divines and the Puritans this way: "The essence of the King James Bible lies precisely in the coming together of these mentalities, the enriched substance of [Lancelot] Andrewes's supremely well-stocked mind lit by the fierce white light of Puritanism."[40]

All were ordained clergy except one: Sir Henry Savile, who had been Greek tutor to Queen Elizabeth I, and on that basis—plus a flair for self-promotion—he was assigned to the Gospels team.

We know little about the daily doings of the committees, the discussions and disputes that went on behind the scenes. They spent more time together than any coworkers normally would. Occasionally, they took their discussions to the pub. Although the Puritans on the committee must have perceived of some of the divines as dandies, and the divines, in turn, probably viewed some of the Puritans as having more passion than erudition, these fifty men kept each other's confidences and served the greater cause to an astonishing degree. What we don't know is to their credit.

One of their innovations was to identify for the reader the occasional English words they added to the Bible, words that are not in Hebrew or Greek but help clarify the meaning of the original languages. Many translators add such words in order to make things sensible in the new language, and the KJV tells you what they are. These added or "provided" words now appear in italics in most editions. (In the original 1611 edition, these added words were set in lighter, regular letters among darker "gothic"-style type.) So, for example, look at Psalm 7:11 and you can see three words in

---

40. Adam Nicolson, *God's Secretaries: The Making of the King James Bible* (New York: HarperCollins, 2003), 125.

italics; this is a phrase that the translators are telling us is not from the literal Hebrew:

> God judgeth the righteous, and God is angry *with the wicked* every day.

We might be grateful that they added such a phrase! At the same time, had they known linguistics, texts, and ancient Hebrew in the ways that translators do today, they could have solved such a problem with greater understanding of what the original language is trying to say. This is how the Koren *Jerusalem Bible* does it:

> God is a righteous judge; and a God who has indignation every day.[41]

No need to italicize anything.

We know that they sought majestic language as well as language faithful to the original languages. There's one story of a dispute on the committee translating the Epistle to the Hebrews. One of the committee members, the Greek scholar Andrew Downes, argued for a rendering of chapter 13, verse 8 that's different from what was finally produced. Instead of "Jesus Christ the same yesterday, and today, and for ever"—he wanted something with better rhythm and more aural appeal, that would make for a grander benediction: "Jesus Christ, yesterday, and to day the same, and for ever." He lost.[42]

Translation work is not always exciting stuff, but the collaborative way in which those gathered came together is demonstrated in the final product.

---

41. *The Jerusalem Bible*, English text revised and edited by Harold Fisch (Jerusalem: Koren Publishers, 2000). This was the first Bible published in modern Israel and is still the Bible with which all presidents of the State of Israel are sworn into office. Not to be confused with the Roman Catholic Bible of the same name that was introduced in 1966.

42. Adam Nicolson, *God's Secretaries*, 211–12.

After seven years of work, in the spring of 1611, most of the work was done. Before being sent off to the printers, running heads and chapter summaries were added by Bishop Miles Smith of Gloucester. And according to tradition, the politically astute Bishop Thomas Bilson of Winchester penned the dedication to James that opens the great work. A few of the Puritans surely grumbled about it:

> To the Most High and Mighty Prince
> James
> By the Grace of God
> King of Great Britain, France, and Ireland
> Defender of the Faith, etc.
> The Translators of the Bible wish
> Grace, Mercy, and Peace
> Through Jesus Christ our Lord

After such a salutation, Bilson's first sentence reads, "Great and manifold were the blessings, most dread Sovereign, which Almighty God, the Father of all mercies, bestowed upon us the people of England, when first he sent Your Majesty's Royal Person to rule and reign over us."

The KJV that we read today is not that original 1611 edition. In fact, there are scarcely any extant copies. Revisions were made only two years later, in 1613, and again in 1629 and 1638. From the beginning, and over the next century or more, printers' typographical errors and misprints entered into the work. Alister McGrath tells this anecdote:

> The story is told of a bishop who, having been invited to preach around 1675 on a certain biblical text in St. Paul's Cathedral ... went into a nearby London stationer's to buy a London-printed Bible so that he could study the text. On

turning to the appropriate page, he found that the verse had been left out altogether.[43]

London-printed Bibles were notorious for typos, compared to those printed on the Continent. Finally, by the mid-1700s, dissatisfaction grew to the point where serious efforts were made to improve quality and workmanship. Major fixes and revisions were made at Cambridge in 1762, but then, more significantly and thoroughly, at Oxford in 1769. Improvements were also made to the typography, and some spellings were modernized so that they conformed to English usage in those days. Paper quality even improved (the English began importing it). This edition was quickly called the Oxford Standard Edition, and it is used for almost all KJV Bibles in circulation today.

It is the 1769 Oxford Standard Edition that I quote from throughout *Verily, Verily*. See for yourself the dramatic changes from 1611 to 1769, in these simple examples from 1 Corinthians chapter 13:

> 1611: Though I speake with the tongues of men & of Angels, and haue not charity, I am become as sounding brasse or a tinkling cymbal.
> 1769: Though I speak with the tongues of men and of angels, and have not charity, I am become as sounding brass, or a tinkling cymbal.

———

> 1611: And though I haue the gift of prophesie, and vnderstand all mysteries and all knowledge: and though I haue all faith,

---

43. Alister McGrath, *In the Beginning: The Story of the King James Bible and How It Changed a Nation, a Language, and a Culture* (New York: Doubleday, 2001), 214.

so that I could remooue mountaines, and haue no charitie, I am nothing.

1769: And though I have the gift of prophecy, and understand all mysteries, and all knowledge; and though I have all faith, so that I could remove mountains, and have not charity, I am nothing.

—

1611: And though I bestowe all my goods to feede the poore, and though I giue my body to bee burned, and haue not chari-tie, it profiteth me nothing.

1769: And though I bestow all my goods to feed the poor, and though I give my body to be burned, and have not charity, it profiteth me nothing.

1 Corinthians 13:1 – 3

Western culture can be traced through its major books—from Homer and Plato in Greek, to the Vulgate and Thomas Aquinas' *Summa Theologica* in Latin, to the King James Bible and the works of Shakespeare in English—English that's very close to our own. And with the KJV, you might say that English began to become the *new* Greek, the *new* Latin. What has become the world's language was in many ways begun by the influence and reach of the world's Bible.

LO, THE HUMOR!

And the LORD God caused a deep sleep to fall upon Adam,
and he slept: and he took one of his ribs, and closed up
the flesh instead thereof; And the rib, which the LORD God
had taken from man, made he a woman.

GEN. 2:21–22

I followed the other Experiment around, yesterday afternoon,
at a distance, to see what it might be for, if I could.
But I was not able to make out. I think it is a man.

MARK TWAIN, FROM *EVE'S DIARY*

There are verses in the KJV that are grand, soaring, and beautiful. But there are others that are just plain odd, incongruous, hilarious, and earthy. Just as we can't underestimate the seriousness and skill of the KJV translators, we can also recognize that there's much to chuckle at.

WHAT CONFUSED US AS KIDS

Certain KJV words caused giggles in my Sunday school classes as a child. Perhaps they still do. I hope so. Words such as *suffer* or *kid* or

91

virtue or *know* have meanings in the King's English that can easily embarrass us.

Didn't Jesus say, "Suffer little children, and forbid them not, to come unto me" (Matthew 19:14)? Wait a minute. What? Does Jesus want little kids to suffer? Actually, *suffer* means "allow."

And then, of course, there's "Thou shalt not seethe a kid in its mother's milk" (Exodus 23:19) — which might make a child wonder why anyone would be tempted to put kids in milk — and then if they learned that *to seethe* meant "to boil," they'd be scared to death until they discovered that a kid was a young goat. It all starts feeling like an episode of *Are You Smarter Than a Fifth Grader?* after a while.

What boy can keep a straight face as his Sunday school teacher solemnly reads this passage? "[I]t shall come to pass, when my lord the king shall sleep with his fathers, that I and my son Solomon shall be counted offenders" (1 Kings 1:21). That doesn't sound right, until your teacher tells you to quiet down; *sleep* is a euphemism for dying.

Much more seriously, what child wouldn't be seriously confused when they hear this verse — until they learn that *virtue* means "strength"? "And Jesus said, Somebody hath touched me: for I perceive that virtue is gone out of me" (Luke 8:46). I certainly found it funny to imagine what it might have looked like that day, as Jesus was walking near Galilee, and his virtue suddenly fell out of him!

There are plenty of other words that are used in the KJV in different ways than we use them today. Some of these also cause children to snicker and adults to occasionally scratch their heads. Consider *bosom*. What exactly was God asking Moses to do in this passage? "And the Lord said furthermore unto him, Put now thine hand into thy bosom ..." (Exodus 4:6)? The meaning of the word, in this case, is the same as it is in this one from Proverbs: "A slothful man hideth his hand in his bosom, and will not so much as bring it to his mouth again" (19:24). This sort of "bosom" is the folds of clothing in the area around the human breast. The proverb essentially means: If you don't use your hands for working, you're lazy and will probably go hungry! This is quite different from what we would typically expect of the word *bosom* today: "And Naomi took the child, and laid it in her bosom, and became nurse unto it" (Ruth 4:16).

And then there's perhaps the biggest giggler of all: the KJV's Old Testament idiom for "going to the bathroom." This phrase occurs twice and the best instance is this, because, from the scene, it's almost clear what the idiom means without someone having explained it to you beforehand: "And it came to pass, when Saul was returned from following the Philistines ... he came to the sheepcotes by the way, where was a cave; and Saul went in to cover his feet ..." (1 Samuel 24:1, 3).

"HE STINKETH"

Some of the humor in the KJV comes from what I'd call its earthiness. Sometimes those divines and Puritans knew how to paint a picture just right. They sometimes told it straight and bluntly about matters that we tend to sanitize today.

I'm thinking of the occasion in John's gospel when Jesus raises his friend Lazarus from the dead. Lazarus has been lying dead in the tomb — "a cave, and a stone lay upon it" — for four days by the time Jesus arrives. That's a long time ... so long that the guys on *CSI* would don serious masks before sneaking a peek.

But Jesus says to the people gathered nearby, "Take ye away the stone."

Martha, the sister of Lazarus, steps forward and offers a mild protest. Imagine what she must be thinking. Without missing a beat, Martha interjects: "Lord, by this time he stinketh" (John 11:39).

Stinketh indeed! We have no trouble imagining the truth her words represented. The only other time the word "stinketh" occurs in the KJV comes in Isaiah 50:2 — and it refers to fish. Lots of today's translations are more sanitized and, as a result, less interesting. The NIV accounts for a "bad odor" around Lazarus's tomb, which is pretty good, but the NRSV only has Martha offering that "there is a stench." Much of the frankness and earthiness are missing.

Another example of earthy language in the KJV comes in 1 Samuel 25:21 – 22, when King David describes his enemies in a way that distinguishes them as distinctively male. David says,

> Surely in vain have I kept all that this fellow hath in the wilderness, so that nothing was missed of all that pertained unto him: and he hath requited me evil for good. So and more also do God unto the enemies of David, if I leave of all that pertain to him by the morning light any that pisseth against the wall.

This isn't to be found in modern translations. The NRSV translates the same Hebrew phrase — referring to something that only men can do — by simply avoiding it: " ... if by morning I leave so much as one male of all who belong to him."

"ME TARZAN, YOU JANE"

Four hundred years of distance have made some of the more archaic words and phrases of the KJV downright hilarious. For example, it might just be possible that caveman talk got its start right there at the beginning of Genesis. Seriously! Consider this. What does Adam say immediately after God has created Eve in Genesis chapter 2?

Adam has just concluded naming all of the beasts of the air and sea and land. Then God sets about creating this new and much more phenomenal creature out of Adam's side. She must have been something to behold for the first man who had only seen four-legged, swimming, and flying things. Genesis records:

> *And Adam said, This is now bone of my bones, and flesh of my flesh: she shall be called Woman, because she was taken out of Man.*
>
> GENESIS 2:23

I can't hear those words without thinking of the beginnings of caveman talk. It's as if the first man said, while pounding his chest, sticking out his chin with great aplomb: "She, Wooo-mahn! Me, Maaahn!"

Linguists date the invention of written language to sometime around 5,000 years ago — the millennium before the birth of Abraham and Sarah. What comes before that is what we know as the "prehistoric era," which is also called the "me Tarzan" stage by some of the experts.[44] I propose that we call it, instead, the Garden of Eden, or "She, Wooo-mahn," stage!

Could it be that the first evolutionary theorists looked to the King James Bible for their inspiration as to how early *Homo sapiens* talked about women? It's *possible*.

At the other end of the Bible, in the Book of James, there's an equally intriguing example of how a sentence in today's more recent translations is meant to be so very forthright but sounds a bit silly

44. Guy Deutscher, *The Unfolding of Language: An Evolutionary Tour of Mankind's Greatest Invention* (New York: Metropolitan Books, 2005), 8–9.

in the original Authorized Version. The verse goes like this in the
NIV:

> *Above all, my brothers, do not swear — not by heaven or
> by earth or by anything else. Let your "Yes" be yes, and
> your "No," no, or you will be condemned.*
>
> JAMES 5:12

In other words, be decisive, and speak your mind! But in the
KJV it reads:

> *But above all things, my brethren, swear not, neither by
> heaven, neither by the earth, neither by any other oath:
> but let your yea be yea; and your nay, nay; lest ye fall
> into condemnation.*

It's pretty tough today to bring off a "nay" or a "yea" with a
sound of authority. It would certainly be tough to say it with aplomb
or while pounding one's chest.

And there's plenty more to chuckle at. There are, for example, a
variety of odd idiomatic phrases that have their origins in the KJV
and some that may surprise you.

"Strain at a gnat" comes from Matthew 23:24–25:

> *Ye blind guides, which strain at a gnat, and swallow a
> camel. Woe unto you, scribes and Pharisees, hypocrites!
> for ye make clean the outside of the cup and of the plat-
> ter, but within they are full of extortion and excess.*

And "flies in the ointment" comes from Ecclesiastes 10:1:

> *Dead flies cause the ointment of the apothecary to send
> forth a stinking savor: so doth a little folly him that is in
> reputation for wisdom and honor.*

The idiom "to see the handwriting on the wall" originates ominously from Daniel chapter 5. This passage has captured a lot of imaginations in the last four hundred years. For one, Rembrandt created a famous painting of the scene, called *Belshazzar's Feast*, in which King Belshazzar looks understandably scared out of his wits.

> *In the same hour came forth fingers of a man's hand, and wrote over against the candlestick upon the plaster of the wall of the king's palace: and the king saw the part of the hand that wrote. Then the king's countenance was changed, and his thoughts troubled him, so that the joints of his loins were loosed, and his knees smote one against another. The king cried aloud to bring in the astrologers, the Chaldeans, and the soothsayers. And the king spake, and said to the wise men of Babylon, Whosoever shall read this writing, and shew me the interpretation thereof, shall be clothed with scarlet, and have a chain of gold about his neck, and shall be the third ruler in the kingdom.*

It's pretty funny to imagine how "the joints of his loins were loosed" and "his knees smote one against another" — because it sounds like a fancy way of saying that his knees were knocking and he almost peed in his pants. But even more interesting, a passage like this one makes me think that perhaps H. P. Lovecraft and Stephen King read their King James Bibles when they were boys. I'll bet that they did, and that horror stories and weird tales began with Scripture.

So did spooky things in the night ...

> *And when the sun was going down, a deep sleep fell upon Abram; and, lo, an horror of great darkness fell upon him.*
>
> GENESIS 15:12

The grim side of life and the darkness in the here and here-after were all easier to imagine four hundred years ago, compared to today. We tend to want things much sunnier. But in a beautiful passage from Psalm 121, God is actually compared to a kind of dark-ness, providing quiet and cool relief from the sun: "The LORD is thy keeper: the LORD is thy shade" (Psalm 121:5).

OUT YOUR NOSTRILS

Some of the humor in the KJV is gross. You might recall the story of the Israelites wandering in the wilderness. Led by Moses, they wander for forty years. God had promised them a land where milk and honey flowed freely. Pillars of fire and cloud lead them on their way. They watch an entire sea open up before them, and they even-tually escape Pharaoh's men while walking on the bed of the sea from one end to the other.

Miraculously, these Israelites are free at last from the chains of Pharaoh and the sneers of the Egyptian people. And yet before long they begin to feel that they're living like escaped convicts or refugees without homes. Men, women, and children are waiting for the Promised Land, and they begin to get hungry. They are almost literally starving when they ask God for help. God graciously gives them manna—miracle food—from heaven.

Each morning, as the sun burns the dew off the ground, this miraculous food appears. The Book of Numbers says that manna arrived in the night, and Exodus adds that, like the dew, it evapo-rated in the heat of the sun, so the people needed to gather it up quickly. It tasted like honey and fell from the sky, day after day, pro-viding the people's needs for sustenance in the midst of an unfor-giving wilderness.

Oh, but it becomes boring. This is when they begin to complain.

The Red Sea opening like a tin can before their eyes wasn't enough. Miracle food delivered to their doorsteps each morning like dew wasn't enough. After a while, they've had so much manna that it becomes boring, day after day. Perhaps they simply need condiments.

Now take up your KJV and revisit Numbers chapter 11. In response to the complaints about manna, this is actually what the Lord says to Moses:

> *Say thou unto the people ... Ye shall not eat one day,*
> *nor two days, nor five days, neither ten days, nor twenty*
> *days; But even a whole month, until it come out at your*
> *nostrils, and it be loathsome unto you.*
>
> NUMBERS 11:18-20

Now we know where our parents got it! *You want to complain about your green beans again, mister?! In that case, you have to eat twice as many. I'll make you eat them until they come out your nostrils!!*

MORE SURPRISES

The KJV also chronicles what must be the earliest example of child delinquency and trouble-making in the history of literature: the gang of kids who taunted the prophet Elisha. Second Kings 2:23 records:

> *And he went up from thence unto Beth-el: and as he was*
> *going up by the way, there came forth little children out*
> *of the city, and mocked him, and said unto him, Go up,*
> *thou bald head; go up, thou bald head.*

Our translators were simply following Tyndale in this case, and their rendering has been followed by most translators ever since.

About the child delinquency, Solomon might say there's nothing new under the sun. (Except that Elisha responds to their mocking by cursing the children and then "two she bears [come] out of the wood, and tare [or maul to death] forty and two ... of them"!)

Other parts of the KJV can also take today's reader by surprise. Some of the proverbs, for instance, can be incongruous and shocking. Consider this one:

> My son, hear the instruction of thy father, and forsake
> not the law of thy mother:
> For they shall be an ornament of grace unto thy head,
> and chains about thy neck.
>
> PROVERBS 1:8–9

Check for yourself if you don't believe me. That's exactly how Proverbs 1:8–9 will appear in your KJV. It seems to be suggesting that a mother's advice is like a chain around your neck. A ball and chain? I swear that I never thought of my mom like that! Modern translations have cleared up the confusion; in the NIV those chains are "to adorn your neck," and in the NRSV they aren't chains at all, but "pendants." Whew!

There are even bad drivers in the Bible:

> And the watchman told, saying, . . . the driving is like the
> driving of Jehu the son of Nimshi; for he driveth furiously.
>
> 2 KINGS 9:20

But the NIV does it even better, saying, "he drives like a madman."

This one may also shock you:

> Men do not despise a thief, if he steal to satisfy his soul
> when he is hungry.
>
> PROVERBS 6:30

It reminds me of the scene in Woody Allen's *Radio Days* where a husband tries to convince his wife that it's okay for the maid to steal from them because, if she didn't, "Who *would* she steal from, if not *us*?"

And then, I find this indictment of laziness to be completely without sting:

> *The slothful man saith, There is a lion in the way; a lion*
> *is in the streets.*
>
> PROVERBS 26:13

That seems like a pretty good excuse for lollygagging to me!

In terms of subject matter, from Mel Brooks to Monty Python to Harold Ramis, many a Hollywood film director has looked to the Bible and found some really good material. And for one raised on the KJV, I can't help but hear its cadence in the occasional movie line, as in *The Godfather* when Sal Tessio says that "Luca Brasi sleeps with the fishes," meaning, he's dead. Doesn't that sound a whole lot like the Old Testament: "And Jehoahaz slept with his fathers; and they buried him in Samaria ..." (2 Kings 13:9)?

UNINTENDED HUMOR

There are also examples of fairly serious errors that appeared in the KJV as copyists, typesetters, and publishers worked with the text over time. In the history of English language Bibles, there have been many occasions when one word or phrase, or even a misplaced comma or small typo, has made for misunderstanding, minor blasphemy, or unintended humor.

One of the more famous examples of this was also the first, and it's called "The Judas Bible." In one of the first printed editions of the KJV, Matthew's gospel has Judas, not Jesus, speaking to the disciples, telling them that he's going to go pray. "Then cometh Judas with them unto a place called Gethsemane, and saith unto the disciples, Sit ye here, while I go and pray yonder" (26:36). That's a problem!

And then there's what's called "The Adulterous Bible" of 1631, also known as "The Wicked Bible," for its printer, Robert Barker, who mistakenly omitted an important negative from Exodus 20:14. As a result, the seventh commandment reads, "Thou shalt commit adultery." If you find one of these Bibles in your attic, hold onto it, because it's really valuable. Only eleven copies of this Bible are known to exist today, as the English government immediately recalled and destroyed the rest.

Innocent mistakes are common in books of all kinds, but today's Bible publishers employ so many proofreaders as to make mistakes almost entirely impossible. It wasn't always so.

The so-called "Vinegar Bible" is one of the more unfortunate early editions of the KJV, in that it was a gorgeous production, one of the most beautiful of its time. Approximately five inches thick, this Bible was 19 ½ inches tall by 12 ¾ inches wide, printed at Oxford University by John Baskett in 1717. But it was full of small typos, none of which were severe enough to condemn the printers, but sufficient to show their carelessness. In the headline above Luke chapter 20, rather than "The Parable of the Vineyard," it reads, "The Parable of the Vinegar."

Sometimes these typos were inserted deliberately, as is likely the case in what's called "The Printer's Bible," an edition of the KJV that appeared around 1700. Psalm 119:161 read: "Printers have persecuted me without cause" rather than "Princes have persecuted me without a cause." The theory goes that a typesetter, at the last moment, changed the word as a passive/aggressive recourse against the greedy printers/publishers who had taken advantage of him.

Similar theories have been floated for an edition published in 1716 in which John 8:11 reads, "Go and sin on more" rather than "Go, and sin no more." Could this have been an instance of a playful copyist having some fun? In any case, religious authorities found little humor in these sorts of mistakes.

"The Fool's Bible" of 1763 has the psalmist saying, "The fool hath said in his heart, There is a God," rather than "The fool hath said in his heart, There is no God" (Psalm 14:1). It's tempting to suspect that a rogue atheist was hiding somewhere in the typesetter's office. Today, perhaps we should call the one that Dawkins/Hitchens Bible? In any case, the printers themselves couldn't have been happy with what always happened next; they would be fined enough to send them to debtor's prison, and every available copy destroyed.

All of these hilarities, oddities, and typos add to the lasting effect of the KJV. To my mind, they argue for its enduring appeal. What fun!

I remember one more verse that made me laugh long ago. There was a time as a child when I believed that this verse from Proverbs gave me permission to ignore my mother's injunction to comb my hair each morning:

> The hoary head is a crown of glory, if it be found in the way of righteousness.
>
> PROVERBS 16:31

I thought that "hoary" meant something like "messy hair," until, of course, I learned that "hoary" simply means venerable, old, and gray.

THE KJV ENDURETH FOREVER

Blessed is he that readeth,
and they that hear the words of this prophecy,
and keep those things which are written therein:
for the time is at hand.

REVELATION 1:3

But the word of the Lord endureth for ever.
And this is the word which by the gospel
is preached unto you.

1 PETER 1:25

The KJV quickly became the official Bible of the Church of England, despite the fact that, after commissioning the Bible in 1604, King James somehow neglected to issue a decree to officially "authorize" this Authorized Version once it was published! But becoming the official Bible of the English church didn't mean that it was instantly popular. The majority of people didn't even notice that a new Bible had been produced to such glorious effect. There was no launch party or book-signing tour.

Most people, in fact, continued to prefer the Geneva Bible, especially the Puritans. It was the one they knew best. Such notable English writers as John Donne, John Milton, and John Bunyan continued to opt for the Geneva well after the KJV was widely available (Donne and Milton warmed to the KJV somewhat in later life, but Bunyan never did). Some Geneva Bibles were printed in England, though as late as the 1640s, editions of the Geneva were still being printed in Amsterdam with fraudulent listings of "London" on their title pages, intended to fool some into thinking the Geneva had been approved for general use in England.

It would be a quarter century before King Charles I (the son of James I) and his Archbishop William Laud pushed laws through Parliament that forbade the publication of the Geneva Bible in England. Like his father, Charles didn't like the Geneva's study notes, nor did he like how the less moderate Puritans refused to use King James's Bible. Charles was willing to go to almost any lengths to make the KJV the only Bible for England. In fact, he went so far as to provoke a civil war.

THE WAR BETWEEN THE BIBLES

The English Civil War (1642–51) was understood by some as the battle of Geneva-readers against KJV-readers: Puritans against the established Church of England; the people against the monarchy; parliamentarians versus royalists. A contemporary newspaper cartoon might have featured a King James Bible with legs and arms in fisticuffs against an opposing Geneva Bible.

Charles I did a variety of things that caused the Puritans and their supporters to worry that England was drifting back toward Catholicism: he married a Catholic woman from one of the royal families of France; he allied himself closely with Archbishop Laud (who was virulent and sometimes violent over his insistence that Puritans fall into line with the Church of England); and he insisted that the churches use only the KJV.

All of this led to Civil War. This intrareligious conflict had a variety of outcomes. At first, the Puritans emerged victorious. In 1645, William Laud was executed in the Tower of London upon the orders of a new, Puritan-led British Parliament, and Charles I was himself beheaded four years later. Oliver Cromwell's Puritan government replaced the monarchy by the end of 1653. But by 1660 the monarchy was back in place — permanently this time — beginning with the return from exile and crowning of King Charles II.

There was a great deal of talk during those tumultuous Civil War years that revisions needed to be made to the KJV. Perhaps modest compromises could be reached between the Bibles. Puritans wanted to get rid of words like "bishop," and there were even editions published in London of the KJV text together with the Geneva Bible's study notes. But with the return of the monarchy, the people of England eventually united around the KJV, regardless of their other sympathies. Many of the remaining Puritans left the country for the American colonies. Soon after the English Civil War ended, the Geneva Bible became a symbol of dissension and instability, and the KJV, of the restored glory of England.

By the close of the seventeenth century, the majority of English Christians recognized only one translation of the Bible: the King James. In 1755, Dr. Johnson, in his preface to his *Dictionary of the English Language*, wrote that he used "the translation of the Bible" as a source — as if there were only one. The other versions, for all practical purposes, had ceased to exist.

Over the next century, the KJV would become an essential

export and a tool for showing the world what it meant to be both English and Christian. If it weren't for the expansionist desires of the English people, leading them to start colonies all over the globe, the KJV may never have attained the status that it did.

Four years before the original 1611 KJV, the English had founded their first colony in the Americas, at Jamestown in 1607. The King's Bibles flowed into Virginia within months of their first publication. By 1670, King Charles II granted a charter to the Hudson's Bay Company and began exporting many things (including Bibles) to Canada. The English were also well onto the other side of the globe and into India by this time. And by 1672, KJVs were accompanying the English slave ships of the Royal African Company to the West Indies. Part of the KJV's history is the way in which a masterful and appealing Bible helped to pave the way for the colonizing era in English history.

THE KJV-ONLY MOVEMENT

As common as the KJV became in England and its colonies, it was still a long way from what later became known as the "KJV-only movement." You probably know someone who holds this view, that the King James Bible is the truest, purest, and best Bible version of all time. A true Christian, assert proponents, cannot use anything else. This movement began in the 1880s, as a reaction against what was the first major translation project undertaken to revise the KJV. The Revised Version was introduced in stages between 1881–85. By 1923, we hear a popular English professor at Yale College make this incredible statement: "We Anglo-Saxons have a better Bible than the French or the Germans or the Italians or the Spanish; *our English translation is even better than the original Hebrew and*

Greek. There is only one way to explain this; I have no theory ... to account for the so-called 'inspiration of the Bible,' but I am confident that the Authorized Version was inspired."[45] The pitch of the KJV-only movement reached its peak in the 1950s when another new translation, the Revised Standard Version, was released.

There will always be those who don't want things to change—recall that even St. Jerome faced resistance when he undertook to translate the Bible into Latin. Change does not mean that we must reject whatever good already exists; a handful of phrases from the Latin Vulgate persist in our religious vocabulary. There's *Ecce homo* ("Behold the man"), *Deo gratias* ("Thanks be to God"), *Pater noster* ("Our Father"), and *Imago Dei* ("The image of God"). Good things endure.

Only one generation after William Tyndale, and a few years before the KJV was underway, a movement was in place to republish the Latin Vulgate. To give vernacular Scripture to ordinary people was like throwing pearls to swine, they said, quoting from a teaching of Jesus (Matthew 7:6). This traditionalist response was published in 1598, approved personally by Pope Clement VIII. That edition remained the standard one for the Roman Catholic Church until the first decade of the twentieth century when Pope Pius X undertook a new one. Even today, there are publishers, such as Maximus Scriptorius Publications (churchlatin.com), who bring out new editions of classic Vulgates. Their motto is "The Latin language is not dead; but it has perished somewhat in the hearts and minds of the faithful. Latin does not need to be resuscitated, but the faithful do."

Sometimes the quest to preserve what is good and precious

---

45. William Lyon Phelps, *Human Nature in the Bible* (New York: Charles Scribner's Sons, 1923), 2. Emphasis mine.

leads people to reject anything new. Seemingly small changes—
like rearranging pews—can turn a congregation upside down.
Perhaps no area of church life is as freighted with passion as one's
preferred version of the Bible.

Every translation since the KJV era has attempted, in one
respect or another, to speak to modern readers. To some Christians, this smacks of giving in. My grandfathers would have pealed
an *amen!* to the idea of standing fast on the KJV, but the average
Christian today has little reason to consider the small differences
between English Bible versions worth fighting for or sufficient to
dictate doctrine.

In truth, not even the KJV translators themselves believed that
the KJV was the single worthy translation of the Word of God.
Nowhere do they claim that. And so the KJV-only crowd of today
cannot claim faithfulness to the vision of the original translators. Many of today's most prominent evangelicals—men whom
you might think would be traditionalist enough to advocate KJV-
only—don't. Evangelicals as diverse as Billy Graham, James Dob-
son, and Carl F. H. Henry haven't taught that the KJV is the only
true translation for at least a few decades now. In the Rev. Jerry
Falwell's first decade at Liberty University, other translations were
endorsed. Even C. I. Scofield, a great champion of the KJV (and my
grandfathers' preferred interpreter of the Scriptures), wrote in one
of his thousands of footnotes to his once-popular Scofield Reference Bible:

> The writers of Scripture invariably affirm, where the subject
> is mentioned by them at all, that the words of their writings
> are *divinely taught. This, of necessity, refers to the original docu-
> ments, not to translations and versions*; but the labours of com-
> petent scholars have brought our English versions to a degree

of perfection so remarkable that we may confidently rest upon them as authoritative.[46]

Yet the KJV-only movement is still alive and kicking. Why? Where does this come from? Their perspective may be stated best by that vanguard of American Christian fundamentalism, a religious publishing house founded by Pastor John R. Rice during the Great Depression, named the Sword of the Lord. The first paragraph of their current statement of faith runs like this:

> WE BELIEVE the Bible, the Scriptures of the Old Testament and the New Testament, preserved for us in the Masoretic text (Old Testament), Textus Receptus (New Testament) and in the King James Bible, is verbally and plenarily inspired of God. It is the inspired, inerrant, infallible, and altogether authentic, accurate and authoritative Word of God, therefore the supreme and final authority in all things (2 Tim. 3:16–17; 2 Peter 1:21; Rev. 22:18–19).[47]

The small minority of Christians who hold this view hold it passionately, as if all of the rest of Christian faith rests upon it. Another similar doctrinal statement lays out an even clearer argument for KJV-only:

I. The Inspiration of the Bible

We believe the Holy Scriptures, composed of the thirty-nine books of the Old Testament and the twenty-seven books of

---

46. C. I. Scofield, *The Scofield Reference Bible*, first published in 1917. This footnote appears in connection with 1 Corinthians 2:13. Emphasis added.

47. See swordofthelord.com/whatwebelieve.htm. This is a change from the opinion of John R. Rice himself, who wrote in his tract *Our God-Breathed Book the Bible* that many translations of the Bible are acceptable: "You will find that they are almost word for word the same, chapter after chapter after chapter" (Murfreesboro, Tenn.: Sword of the Lord Publishers, 1958), 28.

the New Testament, are the verbally inspired Word and Revelation of God. The Bible is inerrant, infallible-God-breathed.
The initial miracle of divine inspiration of the original auto-
graphs also extends to the divine preservation of a pure text to
this day. We have, therefore, the very Word of God preserved
through the Hebrew Masoretic Text and the Greek Textus
Receptus. In the English language, the only Bible translated
from the aforementioned texts is the King James Version.[48]

So what exactly are the Masoretic Text and the Greek Textus Receptus? They sound like secret documents that revealed the
precise words of God to the KJV translators alone and have been
unavailable to any translators ever since. In fact, the Masoretic
Text is the Hebrew text of the Old Testament used by translators,
and the Greek Textus Receptus (received text) is the name given
to the best-available Greek version of the New Testament in the
early seventeenth century. Nine-hundred-and-ninety-nine out of a
thousand contemporary Bible scholars will tell you that the current
Hebrew and Greek texts used by Bible translators in the twenty-
first century surpass the Masoretic Text and Textus Receptus in
reliability and proximity to the originals. Some of the manuscripts
available today are five or six centuries older — and therefore more
accurate — than the manuscripts available to the KJV committee.

To be clear, there are no *original* editions of any of the books
of the Bible. The *only* manuscripts we have are copies — "received
texts." Using the oldest, most reliable texts available is what every
good translator does, so it is only natural that each new translation
should draw on the best available documentation for its sources.

---

48. Accessed in June 2009 at feasite.org/Tracts/fbcdoctr.htm, which was also easily navigated
    to, from the homepage of the Fundamental Evangelistic Association: feasite.org (under
    construction as of August 2010).

Nevertheless, it is important to note that every new textual discovery over the last four hundred years has revealed that the differences between the source manuscripts nearly always involve minor variations of emphasis and word order. Unfortunately for Dan Brown and other conspiracy hypers, no missing books have been discovered, and nothing that scholars have discovered in the past century and a half casts doubt on any major doctrine of or claim about the Bible.

The bottom line is this: the KJV is as reliable as any good modern translation, and—this is what KJV-only proponents fail to understand—any good modern translation is as reliable as the KJV. Crucially, no translation, whether KJV or contemporary, has passed directly from God's mouth to our page; each is a "received text," and each faithfully teaches the story of Yahweh and the gospel of Jesus Christ.

VERILY VERILY

Which brings us to the title of this book. "Verily verily" is the way Jesus, in the KJV, says that the Word of God is reliable. The KJV translators use the phrase twenty-five times, all in the Gospel of John. Other translations have used "amen amen," "truly truly," "most certainly," and a few others.

The original Greek literally means "this is firm," or "trustworthy," or simply "truly." That same word, when uttered by others, is usually translated as the Hebrew word *amen*. The KJV renders the Greek word *alethos* into English as "verily," taking their inspiration from the Latin word *veritas*, which simply means "truth." In the KJV, "verily verily" is a distinctive way that Jesus says God cannot tell a lie. Jesus, as the man of truth, always speaks the very stuff of reality. The Bible is as true and reliable as the heat of a raging fire or the keen edge of an axe. It is as if Jesus, in John's Gospel, begins all his statements by saying, "Listen, you can trust what I'm about to say."

Most French translations render the phrase as *en vérité*, while most Spanish translations use *de cierto*, both of which mean "in truth." Martin Luther's German translation used *wahrlich, wahrlich,* which means "truly, truly," or "verily, verily."

Verily is a word that actually performs what it means. It's a word that has action, making the words that follow it more immediate. Kind of like yelling "Stop!" — *verily* is supposed to cause us to do something.

The KJV translators made one *verily* into two for even greater emphasis. *Verily verily* became their best expression for, "Pay attention — this is reality!" These verilies are a piece of genius in the KJV, and they multiplied like rabbits in the hands of the translators of the Gospel of John. They capture what it might have been like to be the Son of God, and to speak like him....

> *Verily, verily, I say unto you, Hereafter ye shall see heaven open, and the angels of God ascending and descending upon the Son of man.*
>
> JOHN 1:51

—

> *Verily, verily, I say unto thee, Except a man be born again, he cannot see the kingdom of God.*
>
> JOHN 3:3

—

Verily, verily, I say unto you, He that heareth my word, and believeth on him that sent me, hath everlasting life, and shall not come into condemnation; but is passed from death unto life.

JOHN 5:24

—

Verily, verily, I say unto you, He that believeth on me hath everlasting life.

JOHN 6:47

I like how they left it up to the Word itself to say what's truest of all.

GREAT LOVERS
OF THIS BOOK

Thy words were found, and I did eat them;
and thy word was unto me the joy and rejoicing of mine heart:
for I am called by thy name, O LORD God of hosts.

JEREMIAH 15:16

Heart. Noun singular.
"The chief part; the vital part. Life."

DR. SAMUEL JOHNSON

More than a century ago, an American Presbyterian minister said, "I am interested in the people who made the Bible, but I am more interested in the people whom the Bible makes, for they show me the fiber and genius of Scripture as no mental studiousness or verbal exegesis can do."[49] I couldn't agree more. What could be more important than the ways the KJV has formed the followers of Christ? We'll look at a few of them in this

---

49. Quoted in T. Harwood Pattison, *The History of the English Bible* (Philadelphia: American Baptist Publication Society, 1894), 222.

chapter, but also, we'll look at a few famous writers and other international figures who simply imbibed the cadence, language, poetry, and beauty of the KJV for their writings and oratory. As others have pointed out before me, from Herman Melville to William Faulkner, some of our greatest writers have been fond of "biblicizing turns of speech"—and no Bible has provided more inspiration for this than the KJV.[50]

Famous fictional characters have even been influenced by the KJV. Take, for instance, Daniel Defoe's bitter island castaway, Robinson Crusoe (in the novel, *Robinson Crusoe*, published in 1719), who randomly opens his Bible (a KJV!) to Hebrews 13:5 and reads, "I will never leave thee, nor forsake thee." As the character then relates,

> Immediately, it occurr'd, That these Words were to me, Why else should they be directed in such a Manner, just at the Moment when I was mourning over my Condition, as one forsaken of God and Man?...
>
> From this Moment I began to conclude in my Mind, That it was possible for me to be more happy in this forsaken Solitary Condition ... and with this Thought I was going to give Thanks to God for bringing me to this Place.[51]

As we take a closer look at some important authors, we won't include William Shakespeare. He's the most famous figure who lived contemporaneously with the creation of the KJV who was most likely *not* influenced by it. He didn't really have the time. He had written most of his plays before 1611, and he died only five years after its publication. Even so, there are some great conspiracy

---

50. Robert Alter, *Pen of Iron: American Prose and the King James Bible* (Princeton, N.J.: Princeton University Press, 2010), 70.

51. Daniel Defoe, *Robinson Crusoe*, J. Donald Crowley, ed. (London: Oxford University Press, 1972 [orig. 1719]), 113.

theories about the Bard sitting on the Psalms translation committee. Don't believe it. There are hundreds of allusions to Scripture in Shakespeare; he lived in the golden age of English discovery of the Bible; but he knew *other* versions.

Although he never worked on the KJV committee, there's evidence that Shakespeare was influenced by the psalmists. In his historical play, *Henry VI*, Shakespeare has King Henry VI of England say:

> God shall be my hope, My stay, my guide, and lantern to my feet.

Psalm 119:105 reads this way in the KJV: "Thy word is a lamp unto my feet, and a light unto my path." Shakespeare wrote *Henry VI* in the early 1590s, nearly twenty years before the KJV was first published, and probably about seventeen years before the Psalms committee turned in their work. Shakespeare was inspired by the Geneva Bible translation:

> Thy worde is a lanterne unto my feete, and a light unto
> my path.

THE PURITANS

As we've seen, the Puritans had no love for the KJV at first. Most of them opposed it, sometimes violently, when it was introduced. The men and women on the Mayflower carried Geneva Bibles. The KJV was seen as an English government publication, and the Puritans were living in self-exile, having left a nation with whom they had deep disputes.

While the Pilgrims created the famous *Bay Psalm Book* (1640) only twenty years after first landing at Plymouth Rock — a collection of fresh, metrical renderings of the complete Book of Psalms, translated from the original Hebrew — they never produced their own translation of the whole Bible, perhaps because they were already beginning to adopt the KJV on its own merits. John Winthrop, whom scholars believe was the first Puritan leader to embrace the KJV, became the governor of the Massachusetts Bay Colony in 1629. Winthrop believed that the Puritans were led to New England in order to create a holy society. In 1630, he preached his famous "City upon a Hill" sermon, expressing the idea that they were called by God into a new covenant to create a New Jerusalem. His text was this famous verse from the KJV's translation of the Sermon on the Mount: "Ye are the light of the world. A city that is set on an hill cannot be hid" (Matthew 5:14).

> We must delight in each other, make others conditions our own, rejoice together, mourn together, labor, and suffer together, always having before our eyes our commission and community in the work, our community as members of the same body. So shall we keep the unity of the spirit in the bond of peace. The Lord will be our God and delight to dwell among us, as his own people and will command a blessing upon us in all our ways, so that we shall see much more of his wisdom, power, goodness and truth than formerly we have been acquainted with, we shall find that the God of Israel is among us, when ten of us shall be able to resist a thousand of our enemies, when he shall make us a praise and glory, that men shall say of succeeding plantations: the Lord make it like that of New England: for we must consider that we shall be as a City upon a Hill, the eyes of all people are upon us.

Over time, the KJV would unite the Christians of the colonies, becoming the Bible of not only the Puritans in New England, but the Presbyterians of Pennsylvania, the Moravians of North Carolina, and the Anglicans of the South.

THE DECLARATION OF INDEPENDENCE

The debates will go on forever over just what influence the Bible and the Christian faith had on the Founding Fathers. Their most important document, the Declaration of Independence, shows that they were at least interested in preserving some biblical ideals, but they did not do it through verbatim quotations from the King's Bible—or any Bible. Some historians argue that, since the early Puritans brought the Geneva Bible with them from England, the Founding Fathers must surely have had that translation in the room during the two signings of the Declaration, but there is no hard historical evidence for that belief.

By the second half of the eighteenth century, there was no more popular book in the American colonies than the KJV. Trade with England was suspended when the War of Independence began in 1776, and as a result, a shortage of Bibles was soon realized. The chaplain of the Continental Congress wrote as part of a 1777 committee proposal: "The use of the Bible is so universal and its importance so great that ... the committee recommends that Congress will order the Committee of Commerce to import 20,000 Bibles." These Bibles never materialized (it would have meant trading with the enemy), but in 1782 the U.S. Congress gave its first permission for the publication of a Bible, the KJV, on these shores. (England had outlawed it—insisting the colonists support the printers of England.)

The Declaration of Independence famously reads: "All men ... are endowed by their Creator with certain unalienable rights, that among these are life, liberty and the pursuit of happiness." One inspiration for this terrific idea was certainly:

> Every man should eat and drink, and enjoy the good of all his labor, it is the gift of God.
>
> ECCLESIASTES 3:13

JOHN NEWTON
(AND OTHER GREAT HYMN WRITERS)

Some of our greatest hymnists borrow key phrases from the King
James Bible. Several from the second half of the eighteenth century shared a genius for creating songs of praise and thanksgiv-
ing that sounded as if they were plucked directly from the pages
of the KJV. For instance, "O God Our Help in Ages Past," by
Isaac Watts (1674–1748), is a metrical paraphrase of Psalm 90
in the KJV.

LORD, *thou hast been our*   O God, *our help in ages past* . . .
dwelling-place in all generations.   WATTS
—PSALM 90:1

For a thousand years in thy sight   A thousand ages in Thy sight are
are but as yesterday when it is past. like an evening gone.
—PSALM 90:4   WATTS

Two others are an interesting study in contrasts: Augustus Toplady and Charles Wesley, two Christian ministers who disagreed
on doctrine. Toplady (1740–78) was a strict Calvinist, believing
that God foreordains each person to heaven or hell, while Wesley (1707–88), along with his brother, John, emphasized free will
and an individual's choice before God. Today we don't recall their
doctrinal stances, however, as much as we cherish the rich words
of their hymns. Toplady's "Rock of Ages" meditates on the broken
body of the crucified Jesus.

Then came the soldiers, and . . .
when they came to Jesus, and
saw that he was dead already,
they brake not his legs: But
one of the soldiers with a spear
pierced his side, and forthwith
came there out blood and water.
—JOHN 19:32–34

Unto thee will I cry, O LORD
my rock.
—PSALM 28:1

Thou art my father, my God,
and the rock of my salvation.
—PSALM 89:26

Rock of Ages

Rock of Ages, cleft for me,
Let me hide myself in Thee;
Let the water and the blood,
From Thy riven side which flowed,
Be of sin the double cure;
Save from wrath and make me pure.

While I draw this fleeting breath,
When my eyelids close in death,
When I soar to worlds unknown,
See Thee on Thy judgement
  throne,
Rock of Ages, cleft for me,
Let me hide myself in Thee.
                    AUGUSTUS MONTAGUE TOPLADY

The beauty of "Rock of Ages" is, in part, how it sounds like it's lifted directly from Scripture. The rhythm is similar and the metaphors are stunning. God is a rock who willingly split himself open to create a place in which we fragile human beings can hide. The hymnist has been inspired by and built upon the texts of the Bible.

Charles Wesley wrote dozens of hymns that are still sung each week in churches around the world; three of the most popular are "Christ the Lord Is Risen Today," "Hark! the Herald Angels Sing," and "O for a Thousand Tongues to Sing." His lyrics and rhythms are infused with KJV language and meters, and they help to keep this language alive in contemporary Christian worship. In the same way, "Great Is Thy Faithfulness" (1923), by Thomas Chisholm, comes directly from Lamentations 3:22–23:

> *It is of the* LORD's *mercies that we are not consumed,*
> *because his compassions fail not. They are new every*
> *morning: great is thy faithfulness.*

> *Great is Thy faithfulness, O God my Father;*
> *There is no shadow of turning with Thee;*
> *Thou changest not, Thy compassions, they fail not;*
> *As Thou hast been, Thou forever will be.*

> *Great is Thy faithfulness!*

"Amazing Grace" (1779), penned by the former slave-ship captain John Newton, provides another example of the ways in which the KJV influenced a generation of our greatest hymn writers. Newton became the pastor of a small church in the village of Olney, England, preaching as a form of penance for what he did as a slave-ship captain. "I live in the company of 20,000 ghosts," Newton tells his young protégé, William Wilberforce, in the 2006 film *Amazing Grace*. The first verse of the hymn takes its inspiration directly from an equally moving passage in the Gospel of John:

But by what means he now seeth,
we know not; or who hath opened
his eyes. . . . Then again called they
the man that was blind, and said
unto him, Give God the praise:
we know that this man [Jesus] is
a sinner. He answered and said,
Whether he be a sinner or no, I
know not: one thing I know, that,
whereas I was blind, now I see.
—JOHN 9:21, 24–25

Amazing grace, how sweet the
*   sound*
That sav'd a wretch like me!
I once was lost, but now am
*   found,*
Was blind, but now I see.
"AMAZING GRACE," VERSE I

These are just a few of the ways that we sing the KJV still today.

EMILY DICKINSON
(AND OTHER GREAT POETS)

Hundreds of poets have praised the KJV, from Walt Whitman to W. H. Auden to T. S. Eliot to Bono. When the New English Bible was first published, Eliot—who was definitely a bit of a crank—famously said that it "astonishes in its combination of the vulgar, the trivial and the pedantic," arguing that every translation to come after the KJV suffers by comparison.[52]

Sometimes the poetry of the KJV is its greatest virtue, as in the spare way that the shortest verse, John 11:35, was rendered:

> Jesus wept.

Compare that with how Martin Luther translated this verse from the Latin when he published his German Bible in 1534:

> Und Jesus gingen die Augen über.
> ("And Jesus' eyes overflowed.")

The KJV's concision has been rightly copied by modern versions, including the NIV, which renders this verse exactly as the King James Version does.

Consider another example of the KJV's poetry: 1 Kings 19:12 and its description of God's presence with the most memorable but simple and poetic phrase that came to stand for a people's hope in God's sometimes elusive guidance and protection:

---

52. T. S. Eliot, *Sunday Telegraph*, no 98 (December 16, 1962): 7.

"a still soft hissing" (Coverdale)
"a small still voice" (Tyndale/Matthew's)
"a still small voice" (KJV)

More recently, this is how three of our most important, contemporary translations have rendered it:

"a gentle and quiet whisper" (The Message) — a simple,
    more contemporary metaphor
"a light murmuring sound" (New Jerusalem) — which
    sounds like an unwelcome annoyance
"a sound of sheer silence" (NRSV) — which seems, to me
    at least, to make no sense at all

I'll take the KJV. And that compactness and punch would be imitated in the verse of the first great American female poet.

Emily Dickinson (1830–86) lived a quiet outward life — but an intense inner one. She was raised in the Congregational Church in Amherst, Massachusetts, but wandered away from it toward the end of her life. She lived close to books and spent many hours reading her personal KJV and the books of theology in her lawyer-father's library. She once wrote:

A *word is dead*
    When it is said,
    Some say.

I say it just
    Begins to live
    That day.

She was a passionate, strong woman, and drawn to the livelier portions of Scripture, particularly the Book of Revelation. In her mind, she imagined the trials of a tested faith and the future rewards that may come. But she also penned poems that were poignantly frustrated with promises in the Bible that she no longer seemed to feel. The judgment of Scripture and the absence of God became two of her persistent themes, as in this verse about the Bible itself:

> *The Bible is an antique Volume—*
> *Written by faded men*
> *At the suggestion of Holy Spectres—*
> *Subjects—Bethlehem—*
> *Eden—the ancient Homestead—*
> *Satan—the Brigadier—*
> *Judas—the Great Defaulter—*
> *David—the Troubador—*
> *Sin—a distinguished Precipice*
> *Others must resist—*
> *Boys that "believe" are very lonesome—*
> *Other Boys are "lost"—*
> *Had but the Tale a warbling Teller—*
> *All the Boys would come—*
> *Orpheus' Sermon captivated—*
> *It did not condemn—*

CHARLES DICKENS

Some writers used the King James Bible to point beyond the text to what a Christian's life is supposed to be about.

In *Bleak House*, Dickens created one of his typical characters: a waif who sweeps for a living, scrounges for food, and lives in an abandoned house. The impersonal narrator of *Bleak House* uses biblical phrases to describe the characters and to pepper their conversations. When we first meet this boy, Jo, the narrator says: "Jo, is it thou? Well, well! Though a rejected witness, who 'can't exactly say' what will be done to him in greater hands than men's, thou art not quite in outer darkness." The point of this novel, as in much of Dickens, is to criticize the aristocracy and the church, the places of power and society, for the ways in which the poor are easily forgotten. To do so with KJV-esque language was Dickens' way of saying: God belongs to these.

In chapter 25 of *Bleak House*, Jo tells another character that he has never heard a word of the Bible, while the Rev. Mr. Chadband prattles on about faith, with language full of the KJV. You can plainly tell that the Rev. will do nothing to seriously help the poor boy.

Dickens knew his Bible well, and Rev. Chadband alludes to phrases from it throughout his speeches (all of his conversations are more like speeches). He even pompously quotes from that beautiful portion of 1 Kings mentioned above where Elijah did not hear God in the strong wind that broke rocks into pieces, nor in the earthquake and fire that followed. Chadband flippantly says, "I hear a voice ... is it a still small voice, my friends? I fear not, though I fain would hope so ... because he is devoid of the light that shines in upon some of us." It is soon after this speech, and other airs put on by the portly Rev., that the narrator tells us that Jo has never heard the Bible, let alone read it, and we find ourselves wishing to be more like Jo than such a clergyman.

FREDERICK DOUGLASS

The fearful reactions shown by many ecclesiastics at the time of Tyndale's first vernacular Bible translations prefigured the reactions of American slave-owners who, when they learned that their slaves were learning to read the Bible in English, responded brutally. They were swift with executions, church burnings, and decrees that Bible reading and even literacy were forbidden. Such is the power of the Word! Church leaders and slave owners alike were afraid. Sadly, one Episcopalian priest boasted, in the days of American slavery, that his church, unlike those of the Methodists, would never allow slaves access to the Bible. He said that in his church slaves "were not allowed to exhort or expound scriptures in words of their own … and to utter … whatever nonsense might happen into their minds."[53] This is part of our inheritance too.

African-American writer and abolitionist Frederick Douglass had a fascinating love-hate relationship with the KJV that makes me mindful of Revelation 10:10:

> And I took the little book out of the angel's hand, and ate
> it up; and it was in my mouth sweet as honey: and as
> soon as I had eaten it, my belly was bitter.

In his autobiography, *Narrative of the Life of Frederick Douglass, An American Slave*, Douglass tells of how Bible reading and Christian practice, learned when he was a slave, could have soured him completely to God:

> Every thing [my master] possessed in the shape of learning or
> religion, he made conform to his disposition to deceive. He
> seemed to think himself equal to deceiving the Almighty. He
> would make a short prayer in the morning, and a long prayer
> at night; and, strange as it may seem, few men would at times
> appear more devotional than he. The exercises of his family

53. Quoted in Allen Dwight Callahan's *The Talking Book: African Americans and the Bible* (New Haven, Conn.: Yale University Press), 9.

devotions were always commenced with singing; and, as he was a very poor singer himself, the duty of raising the hymn generally came upon me. He would read his hymn, and nod at me to commence. I would at times do so; at others, I would not.... Such was his disposition, and success at deceiving, I do verily believe that he sometimes deceived himself into the solemn belief, that he was a sincere worshipper of the most high God.[54]

This is one of the tensions for those of us who love the cultural heritage of the KJV—its difficult past. But Douglass also speaks of first desiring to read because of hearing his master's wife read her Bible.

In 1849, Frederick Douglass engaged in a public debate with another brilliant freed slave, Henry Garnet, over whether or not to raise funds to send Bibles to slaves still captive in the American South. While Douglass argued that the KJV was essentially the tool of the white Southerner used to keep African-Americans in servitude, Garnet argued that the liberating power of the KJV—borne out in certain passages, mostly those that deal with the Israelites getting free from Pharaoh—would be precisely the instrument of inspiration slaves needed in order to free themselves. Both men were right; they recognized as much during their debates; and the contradictions of the Bible on matters of justice have been evident ever since.

AFRICAN-AMERICAN SPIRITUALS

The great spirituals take some of their poignancy from a combination of distinctive dirge-like tunes and the way that they claim portions of the KJV that focus on God's care for the underprivileged

54. Frederick Douglass, *Narrative of the Life of Frederick Douglass, American Slave* (Boston: Anti-Slavery Office, 1845), 39.

and oppressed. The very word *spirituals* was probably inspired by a verse from the KJV:

> *Speaking to yourselves in psalms and hymns and spiritual*
> *songs, singing and making melody in your heart to the*
> *Lord.*

EPHESIANS 5:19

Again and again, these song writers used portions of the KJV to reflect their experiences of captivity, freedom, and anticipation of the heavenly future. They looked often to this beautiful passage from the Psalms:

> *By the rivers of Babylon, there we sat down, yea, we*
> *wept, when we remembered Zion. We hanged our harps*
> *upon the willows in the midst thereof. For there they that*
> *carried us away captive required of us a song; and they*
> *that wasted us required of us mirth, saying, Sing us one*
> *of the songs of Zion. How shall we sing the* LORD's *song*
> *in a strange land?*

PSALM 137:1 – 4

In spirituals, proper nouns like *Babylon* usually become metaphors for captivity, while *Zion* stands for both the freedom of the North and heaven.

The anonymous spiritual "Go Down, Moses" is one of the most famous examples. Words and phrases from the KJV's Book of Exodus abound. The title of the song itself is from "Moses, Go down, charge the people" (Exodus 19:21), and its famous refrain, "Let my people go" is taken directly from Exodus 5:1, and other places in the long story of the Exodus of the Hebrews from Egypt and slavery to Pharaoh.

Wallace Willis was a freed slave who lived in the Indian territory of what is now the state of Oklahoma. He was the author of several famous African-American spirituals, including "Swing Low, Sweet Chariot." The song was first performed by the Fisk Jubilee Singers shortly after they formed, in 1871. Willis said he was inspired by the Red River of the Indian territory, imagining it to be like the River Jordan of the Promised Land. Willis imagined himself and other freed slaves to be like the Prophet Elijah who was blissfully taken, without dying, to heaven in a chariot. The language of the song served also as a code to other slaves, offering them hope; they understood that the "chariot" was also a reference to the cart, or some other conveyance, that could carry them North to freedom.

> *I looked over Jordan and what did I see?*
>   *Coming for to carry me home.*
>   *A band of angels coming after me,*
>   *Coming for to carry me home.*
>
> *Swing low, sweet chariot,*
>   *Coming for to carry me home.*
>   *Swing low, sweet chariot,*
>   *Coming for to carry me home.*

Many famous cultural artifacts, from poems to hymns to speeches, were written by people whose lives were filled with the language of the KJV.

ABRAHAM LINCOLN

Abraham Lincoln may have been one of the first people to say, "I am spiritual but not religious." He didn't say it precisely that way—

because the words *spiritual* and *spirituality* weren't in currency at that time—but Abe and his wife, Mary, rented a pew in the local Presbyterian church in Springfield, Illinois, without ever actually joining up. In fact, he never joined any church, although he read his Bible almost daily, quoted from it at the most critical moments in his life, and attempted to shape his life by its precepts.

Our sixteenth president wasn't pious, but he was a man of the KJV. In 1841, the mother of one of his childhood friends gave him an Oxford KJV Bible, and young Lincoln pledged to read it often and to live by its principles. In 1864, while he was president, some freed slaves gave Lincoln another KJV. He responded by saying: "In regard to this Great book, I have but to say, it is the best gift God has given to man. All the good the Savior gave to the world was communicated through this book. But for it we could not know right from wrong. All things most desirable for man's welfare, here and hereafter, are to be found portrayed in it."[55]

In 1858, while running for the U.S. Senate, he gave his famous "House Divided" speech, framing the argument against slavery around the words of Jesus: A "house divided against itself shall not stand" (Matthew 12:25).

His two most famous speeches—which are perhaps the most famous speeches that any president has ever delivered—are the Gettysburg Address (November 19, 1863) and his Second Inaugural (March 4, 1865). They too are full of the KJV. Consider the most recognized example: "Fourscore and seven years ago ..." Why would he begin the Gettysburg Address in this way, with language that was archaic for its time? Didn't he wish to speak directly to the people in words that they would understand? Yes, of course;

---

55. Abraham Lincoln, *The Collected Works of Abraham Lincoln, Volume 2*, Roy P. Basler, ed. (New Brunswick, N.J.: Rutgers University Press, 1974), 542.

but Lincoln was talking to a people deeply divided by war and yet united by a respect for the Bible. He was echoing the language of the KJV. He was, in fact, using the language of the KJV because it would be heard by his listeners as the language of God. *Fourscore* appears a total of forty-six times in the KJV, first in Genesis 16:16: "And Abram was fourscore and six years old, when Hagar bare Ishmael to Abram."

Lincoln's fellow Illinoisan, poet Carl Sandburg, once said, "In the Second Inaugural he spoke as an interpreter of the purposes of the Almighty, as a familiar of the pages of Holy Writ."[56] The last paragraph of the Second Inaugural sounds so biblical because Lincoln was trying to heal the wounds of war and bring the country together:

> With malice toward none; with charity for all; with firmness in the right, as God gives us to see the right, let us strive on to finish the work we are in; to bind up the nation's wounds; to care for him who shall have borne the battle, and for his widow, and his orphan—to do all which may achieve and cherish a just, and a lasting peace, among ourselves, and with all nations.

Lincoln's humor was legendary long before he lived in the White House. In his famous debates with Stephen Douglas in 1858, Douglas would complain that Lincoln quoted from the Bible too often in making his points. On one occasion, Lincoln did just that in order to counter Douglas's belittling of popular sovereignty as the way for new states joining the Union to determine for themselves whether or not to allow slavery. Lincoln used one of the "verily" passages to tell the crowd that Douglas was acting like God:

---

56. *Lincoln's Devotional*, introduction by Carl Sandburg (Great Neck, N.Y.: Channel Press, 1957), viii.

He says I have a proneness for quoting scripture. If I should do it now, it occurs that perhaps he places himself somewhat upon the ground of the parable of the lost sheep which went astray upon the mountains, and when the owner of the hundred sheep found the one that was lost.... The application is made by the Savior ... thus, "Verily, I say unto you, there is more rejoicing in heaven over one sinner that repenteth, than over ninety and nine just persons that need no repentance." And now, if [Douglas] claims the benefit of this parable, *let him repent*.

The crowd roared with laughter.[57]

MARK TWAIN

Mark Twain was always stirring up trouble, and he was nearly always funny. He was raised in a home and church that were fundamentalist and traditional regarding biblical truth. He grew up being schooled in the KJV. But it was Twain who once said that if Christ were here today, he certainly wouldn't be a Christian. (Sometimes some of us might agree.) He was a critic of the institutional church but a fan of following Jesus, long before anyone thought of words and phrases like *post-denominational*.

Twain's character, Tom Sawyer, had much in common with his creator, only Tom was shorter and younger. In chapters 4 and 5 of *Tom Sawyer*, Tom lies about having memorized nearly 2,000 verses from Scripture, only to be embarrassed by Judge Thatcher, who asks him to name two of the apostles and Tom comes out with "David and Goliath!" Before that happens, his cousin Mary tries to help him with the memorization:

---

57. Quoted in Lincoln, *Collected Works of Abraham Lincoln*, Vol. 2, 510–11.

Mary took his book to hear him recite, and he tried to find
his way through the fog:

"Blessed are the—a—a—"

"Poor—"

"Yes—poor; blessed are the poor—a—a—"

"In spirit—"

"In spirit; blessed are the poor in spirit, for they—they—"

"Theirs—"

"For theirs. Blessed are the poor in spirit, for *theirs* is the
kingdom of heaven. Blessed are they that mourn, for
they—they—"

"Sh—"

"For they—a—"

"S, H, A—"

"For they S, H—Oh, I don't know what it is!"

"Shall!"

"Oh, shall! for they shall—for they shall—a—a—shall
mourn—a—a—blessed are they that shall—they that—
a—they that shall mourn, for they shall—a—shall what?
Why don't you tell me, Mary?—what do you want to be so
mean for?"

Characters like Tom and Huck were the humorist's ways of
showing the wonder of childhood and childishness. But he grew
somewhat darker over time, and toward the end of his life Twain
argued with the KJV with a darker sort of humor.

As an adult, he became what we would call a liberal Christian. His pastor taught, for instance, that Scripture wasn't simply
dictated to the writers by the Almighty. Twain sometimes longed
for the traditional religion of his youth, but was also critical of it.
He once said of the KJV: "It is full of interest. It has noble poetry

in it; and some clever fables; and some blood-drenched history; and some good morals; and a wealth of obscenity; and upwards of a thousand lies."[58]

Late in life, the humorist started having fun with the literal way that some people read the Bible. He wrote the religious satires *Extracts from Adam's Diary*, *Eve's Diary*, and *Adam's Soliloquy*. In the latter, he pokes fun at the idea that dinosaurs were in the Garden of Eden and yet absent from the Bible. He has Adam saying, while walking through New York's Natural History Museum: "It is strange ... very strange. I do not remember this creature.... I have no recollection of him; neither Eve nor I had heard of him until yesterday. We spoke to Noah about him; he colored and changed the subject."[59]

And then, in *Eve's Diary*, Twain begins the autobiographical reflections of the first woman with this: "Saturday. — I am almost a whole day old, now. — I arrived yesterday. That is as it seems to me. And it must be so, for if there was a day-before-yesterday I was not there when it happened."[60] Adam, meanwhile, can't make heads or tails of the new creature, having been asleep, after all, when she was created. In *Extracts from Adam's Diary*, after some days have gone by, Adam says: "She has taken up with a snake now. The other animals are glad, for she was always experimenting with them and bothering them; and I am glad, because the snake talks, and this enables me to get a rest."[61]

58. Mark Twain, *Letters from the Earth* (New York: Harper & Row, 1942), 14.
59. Mark Twain, *The Bible According to Mark Twain*, eds. Howard G. Baetzhold and Joseph B. McCullough (New York: Touchstone, 1995), 120.
60. Mark Twain, *Collected Tales, Sketches, Speeches, & Essays 1891–1910* (New York: The Library of America, 1992), 635, 695.
61. Twain, *The Bible According to Mark Twain*, 281.

CHARLES DARWIN

Metaphors change. There are popular metaphors in English today that didn't exist in 1611. Take metaphors relating to food and eating, for instance. An absurd idea is "half-baked"; an outburst of emotion may have been "fermenting" and "brewing" for quite a while. These aren't metaphors that you'll find in the KJV. On the other hand, the KJV—like the Vulgate—employs metaphors of cosmology, domain, and worldview that map out a place of privilege in the universe for humankind (higher than other creatures), but also metaphors that show us to be subjects of the God of heaven. Many of these don't translate very well today. It is these ways of conceiving the world that Charles Darwin felt the need to reject, and his rejection of them became a rejection of faith itself.

The young Darwin thought he was going to become an Anglican clergyman. He attended Cambridge University with that aim. Until at least the age of twenty-five, and perhaps even until he was about thirty, Darwin was orthodox in his beliefs, which included believing that the King James Bible was a faithful and literal guide to history. He studied natural theology at Cambridge, which was the attempt to use reason—that is, scientific reasoning and—to demonstrate that the Bible was reliable as a guide to history. Natural theology appealed to Darwin in those days because he was already having doubts about the existence of "revealed" truth. It was in this work that Darwin explored the philosophical arguments that many of us explored in college: the ways that philosophers argue for or against the existence of God. Later, he became interested in geology and explored how he might reconcile the account of Noah and the Ark with the geological record he found on various expeditions to places like Cape Town, South Africa, and the Galapagos Islands in the South Pacific.

At the end of his life, he wrote in his *Autobiography*, "I did not then in the least doubt the strict and literal truth of every word in the Bible; I soon persuaded myself that our Creed must be fully accepted. It never struck me how illogical it was to say that I believed in what I could not understand and what is in fact unintelligible."

We now have a more nuanced view of Darwin and the Bible. He was, at times, morally (and not just intellectually) motivated. His skepticism about the Bible also stemmed from his hatred of slavery and a desire to demonstrate that all humans have a "common descent," overturning the popular belief at the time that said the races had different lines of genealogical descent, to support the slavery of one race by another.

The KJV reflects a time when people felt that the world was more easily understood (even if the heavens were not). The earth was "my footstool," saith the Lord (Isaiah 14:17). It was described as "at rest, and is quiet." A relationship with God was vertical, with heaven above and hell "beneath," as in underground, beneath thy feet (Isaiah 14:7, 9). The psalmist could pray, "Bow down thine ear, O LORD, hear me" (Psalm 86:1) and the people knew that, visible or invisible, their God was in the sky. What was under our feet seemed fairly straightforward, and what lay above our heads was the spiritual, but realistic, unknown. These are the metaphors of an earlier age. To value the cultural heritage of the KJV includes acknowledging that its worldview (no fault of the translators) has led some to question its validity.

WILLIAM JENNINGS BRYAN

The most influential U.S. presidential candidate who never succeeded in his runs for office, William Jennings Bryan (1860–1925) was at the center of public debate on most of the issues that were burning during his days. The Democratic nominee for president in 1896, 1900, and again in 1908, he had occasion to give many a speech and many of them have come down to history as the most eloquent ever given. By our standards today, he is a bit of a puzzle; we would have trouble identifying whether he belongs in a red or a blue state. Bryan was a devout Presbyterian who once said in an interview, late in life, that the day of his baptism (at a Cumberland Presbyterian revival meeting) was the most important day of his life. He was a virulent prohibitionist and a famous opponent of Social Darwinism. He was also, however, an outspoken peace activist in world affairs—a dove rather than a hawk—and a populist, one of the most important critics of monopolies and big business (railroad companies, banks), fighting as a lawyer and politician for the rights of individuals against trusts that protected practices of big corporations that harmed the common man. He was called "The Great Commoner."

He was a lover of the King James Bible. Known for the beauty of his speaking voice and the honed cadences of his speeches, Bryan used the KJV to influence public opinion while running for office, and in the hundreds of talks he gave while serving as Woodrow Wilson's Secretary of State. Immediately after losing his last run for the presidency, with his reputation as a world-class orator well-established, he began giving this famous talk, called "The Price of a Soul."

If you will examine the great orations delivered at crises in the world's history, you will find that in nearly every case the speaker condensed the whole subject into a question, and in that question embodied what he regarded as an unanswerable argument. Christ used the question to give force to the thought which he presented in regard to the soul's value.

On one side He put the world and all that the world can contain—all the wealth that one can accumulate, all the fame to which one can aspire, and all the happiness that one can covet; and on the other side he put the soul, and asked the question that has come ringing down the centuries: "What shall it profit a man if he gain the whole world and lose his own soul?"

He's quoting Mark 8:36.

Bryan is largely remembered today as the attorney who prosecuted John Scopes, the Tennessee high school teacher who intentionally violated the Butler Act by teaching evolution to his students in 1925. The defense attorney, Clarence Darrow, was an avowed agnostic; he declared during the trial that the confidence of Bryan and other witnesses for the prosecution, regarding the accuracy of the Bible, was foolish, ignorant, and bigoted. Five days after the Scopes Trial ended, William Jennings Bryan died in his sleep.

MARTIN LUTHER KING JR.

The American Civil Rights Movement mobilized men and women to fight for justice—often by returning to the prophetic language of historic Christianity. This message, carried in large part by Martin Luther King Jr. (1929–68), was the language of the KJV. The story of the biblical Exodus became the central metaphor for the Civil Rights struggles, and "Let my people go" (Exodus 5:1) one of its signal phrases.

Dr. King first became famous as an orator while pastoring Dexter Avenue Baptist Church in Montgomery, Alabama, at the age of twenty-five. It was there that he became the leader of the 1955 Montgomery Bus Boycott, started by Rosa Parks, and eventually of the Civil Rights Movement itself. He was imprisoned twenty-nine times over the course of thirteen short years, and was assassinated in Memphis on April 4, 1968.

Dr. King stands in the august tradition of powerful black preaching in America. Few Americans realize today that even before the Revolutionary War there were famous black preachers in the Colonies. Pastor George Liele (1750 – 1820), one of the better known, spoke to mixed audiences in Atlanta before the United States was formed. In the decades leading up to the Emancipation Proclamation, a famous pastor named John Jasper (1812 – 1901) preached to similar audiences in Richmond, Virginia.

In Dr. King's "I Have a Dream" speech, delivered on August 28, 1963, on the Mall in Washington, he said: "No, no, we are not satisfied, and we will not be satisfied until justice rolls down like waters and righteousness like a mighty stream." The reference is to Amos 5:24: "But let judgment run down as waters, and righteousness as a mighty stream."[62]

He also rang out with "I have a dream that one day every valley shall be exalted, every hill and mountain shall be made low, the rough places will be made plain, and the crooked places will be made straight, and the glory of the Lord shall be revealed, and all flesh shall see it together."[63] He was quoting Isaiah 40:4, which then continues, "Every valley shall be exalted, and every mountain and hill shall be made low: and the crooked shall be made straight,

---

62. Martin Luther King Jr., A Testament of Hope: The Essential Writings and Speeches of Martin Luther King Jr., ed. by James Melvin Washington (New York: HarperOne, 1990), 218-19.
63. Ibid., 219.

and the rough places plain: And the glory of the LORD shall be revealed, and all flesh shall see it together: for the mouth of the LORD hath spoken it."

And in his last speech, "I've Been to the Mountaintop," given the day before his assassination, Dr. King was remembering the life of the man who led the people of Israel:

> Well, I don't know what will happen now. We've got some difficult days ahead. But it doesn't matter with me now. Because I've been to the mountaintop. And I don't mind. Like anybody, I would like to live a long life. Longevity has its place. But I'm not concerned about that now. I just want to do God's will. And he's allowed me to go up to the mountain. And I've looked over. And I've seen the promised land. I may not get there with you. But I want you to know tonight, that we, as a people, will get to the promised land. And I'm happy, tonight. I'm not worried about anything. I'm not fearing any man. Mine eyes have seen the glory of the coming of the Lord.[64]

He knew well the story of the end of Moses' life, read to him from an early age from the KJV family Bible:

> *And Moses went up from the plains of Moab unto the mountain of Nebo, to the top of Pisgah, that is over against Jericho. And the LORD showed him all the land of Gilead, unto Dan, And all Naphtali, and the land of Ephraim, and Manasseh, and all the land of Judah, unto the utmost sea, And the south, and the plain of the valley of Jericho, the city of palm trees, unto Zoar. And*

---

64. Ibid., 286.

> *the* LORD *said unto him, This is the land which I sware*
> *unto Abraham, unto Isaac, and unto Jacob, saying, I*
> *will give it unto thy seed: I have caused thee to see it with*
> *thine eyes, but thou shalt not go over thither. So Moses*
> *the servant of the* LORD *died there in the land of Moab,*
> *according to the word of the* LORD.

DEUTERONOMY 34:1 – 5

Dr. King is a powerful modern example of how the KJV shaped and is still shaping us. Nearly every time that the word *servant* appears in the Old or New Testaments of the KJV it means "slave." It's a confusing blessing. On the one hand, numerous slaves are referred to in Scripture in ways that clearly condone the practice of keeping humans in servitude to a master; on the other hand, Jesus speaks of himself as a servant/slave (Matthew 12:18) and praises the lowliness of the servant/slave as the prime requirement to be one his followers (Matthew 23:11). While some Christians justified their own perpetuation of the slave trade in England and America by using the words of Scripture, other Christians, using words from the very same King James Bible, helped to bring the practice to its knees.

The prophetic language of the KJV helped spur on the Civil Rights Movement and, in fact, taught us about ourselves. The words and cadences of the original translation entered American living rooms for a decade in one of the most tumultuous periods of our last century. King James's old Bible has the power to affect us still today, put to work in the life of someone like Dr. King, but perhaps even more broadly, in the lives of all of us.

IMMORTAL VERSES

English art critic John Ruskin (1819–1900) recalled how, as a child, his mother nourished him with the King James Bible the way we give our kids milk (or television!):

> After breakfast ... I had to learn a few verses by heart, or repeat, to make sure I had not lost, something of what was already known.... It is strange that of all the pieces of the Bible which my mother thus taught me, that which cost me most to learn, and which was, to my child's mind, chiefly repulsive — the 119th Psalm — has now become of all the most precious to me, in its overflowing and glorious passion of love for the law of God.

Ruskin went on to reflect how the KJV impacted his own way of thinking and expressing himself in language:

> Once knowing the 32nd of Deuteronomy, the 15th of First Corinthians, the Sermon on the Mount, and most of the Apocalypse, every syllable by heart, and having always a way of thinking with myself what words meant, it was not possible for me, even in the foolishest times of youth, to write entirely superficial ... English.[65]

---

65. John Ruskin, as quoted in David Norton, *A History of the English Bible as Literature* (New York: Cambridge University Press, 2000), 396–7.

Few of us in modern times can claim to have memorized such massive portions of Scripture! Few of us today have been so impacted by the KJV as Ruskin apparently was.

Many short portions of the KJV, however, have either made it into our collective unconscious, become a part of our worldview, or are otherwise essential to the ways we explain what we believe. Some of these "immortal" verses or passages have become like cultural landmarks, sparked foundational debates, or functioned as turning points in our way of thinking about ourselves, our culture, and our faith. I have selected a few of the best representative examples. Some have accompanying commentary and explanation, and some stand alone—just because I find them wonderful in themselves!

THE FIVE BOOKS OF MOSES

And God saw that it was good.

GENESIS 1:10

This is the first inkling we have of what God thinks about anything. Beginning in Genesis 1:4, we read what God thought of the Creation as it was going on. Again and again, it was good. This expression has been at the center of theological debates for 2,000 years—from Gnosticism to Manichaeism to Catharism, there have been those who want to deny the goodness of the created world and say, instead, that what is created, matter, is less important than what is of mind or spirit.

———

Be fruitful, and multiply.

GENESIS 1:28

This is God's famous first proclamation in favor of procreation. It is often referenced in the debates within those branches of Christianity that forbid the use of contraception by married couples— and we hear it most often in the KJV version.

———

> *And he said, What hast thou done? the voice of thy brother's blood crieth unto me from the ground. And now art thou cursed from the earth, which hath opened her mouth to receive thy brother's blood from thy hand; When thou tillest the ground, it shall not henceforth yield unto thee her strength; a fugitive and a vagabond shalt thou be in the earth.*
>
> GENESIS 4:10–12

Together with the passage that follows, this one has been used to support racism and, centuries ago, slavery. Phyllis Wheatley (1753–84), a freed black slave in Boston, wrote the following line in a poem from 1773: "Remember Christians, Negroes black as Cain, / May be refined and join thy angelic train."

———

> *And Noah awoke from his wine, and knew what his younger son had done unto him. And he said, Cursed be Canaan; a servant of servants shall he be unto his brethren.*
>
> GENESIS 9:24–25

Long known as "The Curse of Ham," or "The Curse of Canaan," these words are spoken by Ham's father, Noah, against Ham's son,

Canaan. Racists have read this passage as God's justification for their opinions about the cursedness of dark skin. Even Frederick Douglass, in his *Autobiography*, didn't try to challenge the premise of this "curse," but rather used another tack, saying that it would soon fade away:

> If the lineal descendants of Ham are alone to be scripturally enslaved, it is certain that slavery at the south must soon become unscriptural; for thousands are ushered into the world, annually, who, like myself, owe their existence to white fathers, and those fathers most frequently their own masters.[66]

—

I have been a stranger in a strange land.

EXODUS 2:22

These are the words of Moses, but they became the inspiration for many a storyteller—including some of the great horror and science fiction writers, including Robert A. Heinlein, author of *Stranger in a Strange Land*, which won the Hugo award for best science fiction novel in 1961. For writers like Heinlein, the verse/phrase becomes a dystopian view of the world around us and a way to communicate the essential strangeness, unsettledness, disjointedness, of human life. In contrast, Malcolm Muggeridge (1903–90) once wrote of this very same verse: "I can remember it so vividly, as almost the first recollection of life, an overpowering feeling that this world is not a place where I really belong.... I don't think any phrase I have ever heard gave me such a sense of poignancy."[67]

---

66. Frederick Douglass, *Narrative of the Life of Frederick Douglass, American Slave* (Boston: Anti-Slavery Office, 1845), 27.
67. Malcolm Muggeridge, *Jesus Rediscovered* (New York: Doubleday, 1969), 174–75.

———

And the LORD said, I have surely seen the affliction of
my people which are in Egypt, and have heard their cry
by reason of their taskmasters; for I know their sorrows;
And I am come down to deliver them out of the hand of
the Egyptians.

EXODUS 3:7–8

The African-American abolitionist preacher, Absalom Jones (1746–1818), made these verses his text in a famous sermon delivered at Philadelphia on January 1, 1808. He paralleled the deliverance of the children of Israel from their captivity and bondage in Egypt with the deliverance necessary for African slaves in American society.

———

I am come down to deliver them out of the hand of the
Egyptians, and to bring them up out of that land unto a
good land . . . a land flowing with milk and honey.

EXODUS 3:8

———

And Moses said unto God, Behold, when I come unto
the children of Israel, and shall say unto them, The God
of your fathers hath sent me unto you; and they shall say
to me, What is his name? what shall I say unto them?
And God said unto Moses, I AM THAT I AM.

EXODUS 3:13–14

Transliterated in Hebrew as *'Ehyeh-'Asher-'Ehyeh*, the famous phrase at the end of this passage has been variously translated into English since 1611. It is one of the most puzzled over and powerful of all the statements of the Almighty in Scripture.

———

> And God spake unto Moses, and said unto him, I am the
> LORD: And I appeared unto Abraham, unto Isaac, and
> unto Jacob, by the name of God Almighty, but by my
> name JEHOVAH was I not known to them.
>
> EXODUS 6:2 – 3

The word *Jehovah* occurs only four times in the KJV as a name for God. This is the first instance. Tyndale was the first to use the word in an English Bible, and then the KJV retained it. *Jehovah* is a phonetic transliteration of two words in Hebrew that refer to the Lord God, and it's constructed in such a way that the unspoken Hebrew name for Lord may be pronounced. The two Hebrew words are *Adonai* and *YHWH*, and the vowels of the former were combined with the consonants of the latter, to create *Jehovah*.

The intention of the KJV was to create a faithful and accurate translation, and some of the ways they achieved this were to match the emphases of the original languages with their English choices. In ancient Israel it was only for the high priest to pronounce God's name, and even then, only on special occasions. The word that Christians often translate as *Yahweh* is also an English creation. *YHWH* in Hebrew is a word without vowels that is never to be uttered. Whereas Tyndale used "Lord God," the KJV chose to use the capitalized form, "LORD God," retaining some of the tremble that was lost in other English renderings.

———

Your sin will find you out.

———

And the LORD spake unto Moses, saying, Make thee two trumpets of silver; of a whole piece shalt thou make them: that thou mayest use them for the calling of the assembly, and for the journeying of the camps.

Principal translator of the KJV, Bishop Lancelot Andrewes preached a sermon on this passage at Hampton Court on September 28, 1606, before both King James and Puritan leaders, in an effort to convince the Puritan Scottish Presbyterians that God had ordained for the king to govern both church (the "assembly") and state ("the camps"). The metaphor of trumpets, according to Andrewes' sermon, comes from the Jewish Feast of Trumpets (Rosh Hashanah). Andrewes was responsible for translating the Book of Numbers at the time the sermon was preached—and he seems to have used his own soon-to-be-implemented translation; the KJV wouldn't be published until five years later.[68]

THE HISTORICAL BOOKS

They fought from heaven; the stars in their courses fought against Sisera. The river of Kishon swept them

---

68. Project Canterbury, the Library of Anglo-Catholic Theology, has a complete transcription of the sermon on their website as of August 2010, anglicanhistory.org/lact/andrewes/v5/misc7.html.

> *away, that ancient river, the river Kishon. O my soul,*
> *thou hast trodden down strength. Then were the horse-*
> *hoofs broken by the means of the prancings, the pranc-*
> *ings of their mighty ones.*
>
> JUDGES 5:20–22

This passage always leaves me breathless. It has a quality unlike most of Scripture, depicting an otherworldly battle scene. Baffling commentators for centuries, these were John Wesley's notes on five words from the beginning of the passage: "*From heaven*—Or, they from heaven, or the heavenly host fought, by thunder, and lightning, and hail—stones, possibly mingled with fire. *The stars*—Raising these storms by their influences, which they do naturally. *Courses*—Or, from their paths, or stations. As soldiers fight in their ranks and places assigned them, so did these."

———

> *Oh my LORD, wherewith shall I save Israel? behold, my*
> *family is poor in Manasseh, and I am the least in my*
> *father's house. And the LORD said unto him, Surely I*
> *will be with thee.*
>
> JUDGES 6:15–16

Referring to this memorable passage, where Gideon pleads that he's unable to do what God wants, and God promises his very presence, Hannah Whitall Smith (1832–1911) once wrote: "'I will be with thee.' To all words of discouragement in the Bible this is the invariable answer."[69]

---

69. Hannah Whitall Smith, *The God of All Comfort* (New Kensington, Penn.: Whitaker House, 2003), 210.

The LORD hath sought . . . a man after his own heart.

1 SAMUEL 13:14

And after the earthquake a fire; but the LORD was not in the fire: and after the fire a still small voice.

1 KINGS 19:12

THE PSALMS

The Psalms have been called "the treasure house of all of Scripture," because in them is contained everything a Christian needs. It once was that any man who wanted to become a bishop in the Church of England was expected to know all of Psalms by heart. The KJV turned the Hebrew poetry of Psalms into English prose and, in the process, saw Christ where the Hebrews had not. The most popular literary critic of our time, who is also Jewish, says, "The King James Psalms ... are familiar, comforting or daunting, and almost continuously eloquent. Yet there is little that is Hebraic about them; they have become marvelous Christian prose poems."[70] These Psalm portions are most memorable for the ways that they speak to human emotion before God.

When I consider thy heavens, the work of thy fingers, the moon and the stars, which thou hast ordained; What is

---

70. Harold Bloom, "Who Will Praise the Lord?" *The New York Review of Books* (Nov. 22, 2007): 21.

*man, that thou art mindful of him? and the son of man,
that thou visitest him? For thou hast made him a little
lower than the angels, and hast crowned him with glory
and honor.*

PSALM 8:3 – 5

While some people today see classic verses such as these as examples of how the Bible was composed with a prescientific worldview, I prefer historian Adam Nicolson's enthusiasm for the poetry. Nicolson refers to these verses as a prime example of what is most lasting about the KJV: "The marvels of this passage consist above all in one quality, or at least in one combination of qualities: an absolute simplicity of vocabulary set in a rhythm of the utmost stateliness and majesty.... The characteristic sound of the King James Bible is ... like the ideal of majesty itself, is indescribably vast and yet perfectly accessible."[71]

———

My God, my God, why hast thou forsaken me?

PSALM 22:1

These words were of course spoken by Jesus Christ from the cross at his crucifixion (Matthew 27:46). No other translation of this Hebrew sentence would sound quite as appropriate in a made-for-TV miniseries like *Jesus of Nazareth* (1977), Franco Zeffirelli's six-and-a-half-hour masterpiece.

———

71. Adam Nicolson, *God's Secretaries: The Making of the King James Bible* (New York: HarperCollins, 2003), 230–31.

God is gone up with a shout, the LORD with the sound of a trumpet.

PSALM 47:5

———

Have mercy upon me, O God, according to thy lovingkindness: according unto the multitude of thy tender mercies blot out my transgressions. Wash me throughly from mine iniquity, and cleanse me from my sin. For I acknowledge my transgressions: and my sin is ever before me.... The sacrifices of God are a broken spirit: a broken and a contrite heart, O God, thou wilt not despise.

PSALM 51:1–3, 17

Perhaps Dr. Samuel Johnson had this popular passage from the KJV's Psalm 51 in mind when he provided a definition for the word *contrite*, an uncommon word in English today, in his famous *Dictionary* (1755): "Bruised, contrite; worn or broken by rubbing."

———

O LORD my God, thou art very great.... Who laid the foundations of the earth, that it should not be removed for ever.

PSALM 104:1, 5

This verse would become a true turning point in history when Galileo—and others after him—began to publicly challenge the Ptolemaic explanation of the heavens and earth. As an Italian Catholic and reader of the Latin Vulgate, Galileo would have never seen a copy of the KJV. But those who followed in his footsteps would point to this passage in the KJV, and others like it, as they argued against the Bible, saying that the earth *does* move.

———

Happy shall he be, that taketh and dasheth thy little ones against the stones.

Psalm 137:9

There are some awful verses in the Bible, regardless of the translation: there's no getting around it. Most of the awful ones depict awful events without condoning them. This one seems different. This one comes from one of the shortest psalms—one of the violent ones that we never read in church. The speaker represents Israel in exile and is lamenting what has happened to them at the hands of Babylon. In the process, he expresses what the people of Zion would like to do to the children of Babylon. One wonders why *this* didn't go to the Apocrypha!

———

If I ascend up into heaven, thou art there: if I make my bed in hell, behold, thou art there.

Psalm 139:8

One of the most recognized verses of Psalms, this one is also notable as an example of how the first vernacular English Bibles (*and* Shakespeare) created a new place in the cosmic geography: *hell.* The original word in Hebrew is transliterated as *Sheol,* meaning "the place of the dead," or quite literally, where people are buried. The Greek version of the Hebrew Bible, known as the Septuagint (c. 150 BCE, and which the KJV translators used as a primary textual reference point) used the Greek term *Hades*, for rendering the Hebrew *Sheol*. Hades was the Greek god of the underworld. When the Geneva, Tyndale, Coverdale, Bishop's, and KJV Bibles then translated the Greek word as *hell*, they evolved the meaning from a burial place (in the Hebrew) to the underworld (in Greek), to a place of torment (in English), reinforcing ideas of the afterlife that had become common throughout the Middle Ages.

THE OTHER WISDOM WRITINGS

For I know that my redeemer liveth, and that he shall
stand at the latter day upon the earth.

JOB 19:25

Samuel Medley (1738–99), who was a naval man before his conversion, wrote a famous hymn in 1775 based upon this verse, put to memorable music in 1793:

I know that my Redeemer lives;
What comfort this sweet sentence gives!
He lives, He lives, who once was dead;
He lives, my ever living Head.

He lives to bless me with His love,
He lives to plead for me above.
He lives my hungry soul to feed,
He lives to help in time of need.

———

As a dog returneth to his vomit, so a fool returneth to
his folly.

PROVERBS 26:11

—

To every thing there is a season, and a time to every pur-
pose under the heaven:
A time to be born, and a time to die; a time to plant,
and a time to pluck up that which is planted;
A time to kill, and a time to heal; a time to break down,
and a time to build up;
A time to weep, and a time to laugh; a time to mourn,
and a time to dance;
A time to cast away stones, and a time to gather stones
together; a time to embrace, and a time to refrain from
embracing;
A time to get, and a time to lose; a time to keep, and a
time to cast away;
A time to rend, and a time to sew; a time to keep
silence, and a time to speak;
A time to love, and a time to hate; a time of war, and a
time of peace.

ECCLESIASTES 3:1–8

If this passage sounds familiar, chances are that you lived through the 1960s or are a fan of '60s music. These are the lyrics of the Byrds' number one hit single, "Turn! Turn! Turn! (to Everything There Is a Season)," which was composed by folksinger Pete Seeger.

—

Cast thy bread upon the waters: for thou shalt find it
after many days.

ECCLESIASTES 11:1

A signal verse about trusting in God for the future. (As my editor pointed out, however, this really only works metaphorically. In reality, casting bread in water leaves you with soggy bread!) It reminds me of the 1970s hit of the Gospel singing quartet, the Imperials, "Bread Upon the Water." Bass vocalist Armond Morales sang the line from the chorus that beautifully linked this verse with the words of Jesus from Luke 6:38, thereby extending the metaphor: "good measure, pressed down, and shaken together, and running over ..."

———

> Remember now thy Creator in the days of thy youth, while the evil days come not, nor the years draw nigh, when thou shalt say, I have no pleasure in them.... Or ever the silver cord be loosed, or the golden bowl be broken, or the pitcher be broken at the fountain, or the wheel broken at the cistern. Then shall the dust return to the earth as it was: and the spirit shall return unto God who gave it. Vanity of vanities, saith the preacher; all is vanity.
>
> ECCLESIASTES 12:1, 6–8

We could actually include the entire twelfth chapter from the Book of Ecclesiastes as "immortal verses"! This passage has come to represent that day in the future when we will realize the folly of our youth. These verses have inspired many, including Henry James in the title for his 1904 novel, *The Golden Bowl*.

———

> Set me as a seal upon thine heart, as a seal upon thine arm: for love is strong as death; jealousy is cruel as the

grave: the coals thereof are coals of fire, which hath a most vehement flame. Many waters cannot quench love, neither can the floods drown it: if a man would give all the substance of his house for love, it would utterly be contemned.

SONG OF SONGS 8:6 – 7

This has been a popular passage at both Jewish and Christian weddings for thousands of years. As has this one from Ecclesiastes 4:9 – 11: "Two are better than one; because they have a good reward for their labor. For if they fall, the one will lift up his fellow: but woe to him that is alone when he falleth; for he hath not another to help him up. Again, if two lie together, then they have heat: but how can one be warm alone?" Admittedly, a more recent translation might be best used at weddings today.

THE PROPHETS

They shall beat their swords into plowshares.

ISAIAH 2:4

This is the immortal vision of peacemakers seeking nonviolent solutions to conflict. The verse imagines military weapons being transformed into peaceful and productive civilian implements or applications. It's been immortalized in sculpture (in front of the United Nations building in New York City), sermons, speeches, and song lyrics — ranging from the finale of *Les Miserables* to "Heal the World" by Michael Jackson. Inventions such as sonar have been claimed as fulfilling the promise of this verse — sonar was originally invented to detect enemy submarines deep in the oceans, and today is used for medical diagnostic sonography.

———

*In the year that king Uzziah died I saw also the Lord
sitting upon a throne, high and lifted up, and his train
filled the temple. Above it stood the seraphims: each one
had six wings; with twain he covered his face, and with
twain he covered his feet, and with twain he did fly. And
one cried unto another, and said, Holy, holy, holy, is the
LORD of hosts: the whole earth is full of his glory.*

ISAIAH 6:1 – 3

The vision of the prophet, seeing the Lord on his throne sur-
rounded by angelic creatures — "Holy, holy, holy, is the LORD of
hosts: the whole earth is full of his glory" — these verses are one
of the oldest portions of the mass in Christian liturgical traditions,
often called the *Sanctus* (Latin for "holy").

———

*Then shalt thou call, and the LORD shall answer; thou
shalt cry, and he shall say, Here I am.... And the
LORD shall guide thee continually, and satisfy thy soul
in drought, and make fat thy bones: and thou shalt be
like a watered garden, and like a spring of water, whose
waters fail not.*

ISAIAH 58:9, 11

———

*And I will cut off witchcrafts out of thine hand; and thou
shalt have no more soothsayers.*

MICAH 5:12

This verse and several others like it were unique to the KJV as James I had a fascination with, and dread fear of, witchcraft and demonology. He wrote a book on the subject in 1597, and it was rumored to be the king himself who influenced the translators to include the word so frequently in the new translation. In fact, it's believed that Shakespeare wrote his great play *Macbeth* to feed the crown's interests in these occult practices; we know that James carried out witch trials in Scotland before he took the throne of England. The Hebrew and Greek words that are translated "witchcraft" in the KJV are more often rendered "sorcerer," "sorceress," or "murderer" in other translations. References like this one from the prophet Micah became important to the American colonists, such as Cotton Mather, when prosecuting the Salem Witch Trials in 1692.

THE APOCRYPHA

One of the great ironies surrounding today's KJV-only movement is that the 1611 King James Bible included the apocryphal books—without apology. In the previous century, Martin Luther had translated these fourteen short books, but reluctantly, for his own vernacular Bible. Even the Geneva Bible included the Apocrypha. These books were included in the KJV in keeping with article VI of the "Thirty-Nine Articles" of the Church of England: "And the other books ... the Church doth read for example of life and instruction of manners; but yet doth it not apply them to establish any doctrine." The KJV translators were also sure to retain them in order to emphasize how the KJV was to be the Bible for all the people, Protestant *and* Catholic. Nevertheless, their inclusion was yet another reason why the Puritans had trouble embracing the KJV, and within a generation of the first edition of the KJV, the Reformed churches' Westminster Confession (1648) officially removed them from their version of the canon.

———

Give praise to the Lord, for he is good: and praise the everlasting King, that his tabernacle may be builded in thee again with joy, and let him make joyful there in thee those that are captives, and love in thee for ever those that are miserable.

Tobit 13:10

Recited for centuries to uphold the oppression of peoples, including African slaves in early America and Native Americans during the nineteenth century, this is one of the passages of Scripture that does not denounce, but seems to uphold, the order of slaves and masters.

———

And they walked in the midst of the fire, praising God, and blessing the Lord.... Blessed art thou, O Lord God of our fathers: thy name is worthy to be praised and glorified for evermore: For thou art righteous in all the things that thou hast done to us: yea, true are all thy works, thy ways are right, and all thy judgments truth.... O give thanks unto the Lord, because he is gracious: for his mercy endureth for ever. O all ye that worship the Lord, bless the God of gods, praise him, and give him thanks: for his mercy endureth for ever.

The Song of the Three Holy Children 1–4, 67–68

Probably the most famous passage of the Apocrypha, and the most often used in public prayer, these verses (there are 68 in total) tell of praises sung by Shadrach, Meshach, and Abed-nego while they stood unharmed in the fiery furnace of King Nebuchadnezzar. The episode depicts what occurs after Daniel 3:23 and before Daniel 3:24 in today's Roman Catholic and Eastern Orthodox Bibles, where it's usually called "The Song of the Three Young Men."

THE GOSPELS

Ye have heard that it hath been said, An eye for an eye,
and a tooth for a tooth: But I say unto you, That ye
resist not evil: but whosoever shall smite thee on thy
right cheek, turn to him the other also.

MATTHEW 5:38–39

This is not the first time that the Hebrew teaching of "eye for eye" appears in the Bible, but this is the one we remember, for it's this phrasing from the Sermon on the Mount that entered our cultural consciousness. The original teaching comes from the Torah: "And if any mischief follow, then thou shalt give life for life, Eye for eye, tooth for tooth, hand for hand, foot for foot" (Exodus 21:23–24). In 2005, the Colorado Supreme Court overturned the decision of a 1995 Colorado jury in a rape case, after it was shown that members of the jury had copied down this verse and discussed it during deliberations that led to their recommending the death penalty.

———

Seek ye first the kingdom of God, and his righteousness;
and all these things shall be added unto you.

MATTHEW 6:33

You shouldn't feel the slightest bit embarrassed to say the word *ye* when you recite this verse — one of the most beautiful sentences of prose in our language.

Come unto me, all ye that labor and are heavy laden, and I will give you rest.

MATTHEW 11:28

Let them alone: they be blind leaders of the blind. And if the blind lead the blind, both shall fall into the ditch.

MATTHEW 15:14

Another one of those great phrases that long ago entered into everyday use in our language: The blind leading the blind. Just like this one:

Ye can discern the face of the sky; but can ye not discern the signs of the times?

MATTHEW 16:3

The Gospel of Matthew is great for these idiomatic phrases. Some of our most common expressions have their roots in phrases from the KJV version of the first gospel. There's "don't hide your light under a bushel," which is derived from two separate clauses in Matthew 5:15. "Like casting pearls before swine," which comes from a phrase in Matthew 7:6. "Separating the wheat from the chaff," also from two separate clauses of one verse: Matthew 3:12. And "They that take the sword shall perish with the sword" (Matthew 26:52), one of the most common verses used for arguing in support of the death penalty.

Jesus said unto him, If thou wilt be perfect, go and sell
that thou hast, and give to the poor, and thou shalt have
treasure in heaven: and come and follow me.

MATTHEW 19:21

Another turning point in history, this verse inspired Saint Antony of Egypt (c. 251 – 356) to go into the desert and be a monk, living in intentional poverty, devoting himself to prayer and service to others. The entire monastic movement that built Western Christianity throughout the Middle Ages can be traced back to Antony hearing this verse preached in church.

But one thing is needful: and Mary hath chosen that good
part, which shall not be taken away from her.

LUKE 10:42

One of the best KJV phrases in its power of sticking in one's memory! I prefer "One thing is needful" to "but o thing is necessarie" (Wycliffe) or "there is need of only one thing" (NRSV) or "only one thing is necessary" (NASB).

And that servant, which knew his lords will, and pre-
pared not himself, neither did according to his will, shall
be beaten with many stripes.

LUKE 12:47

Another verse that sadly recounts slavery without condemning it. Jesus is telling a parable to a first century audience for whom slavery was a fact of life. Frederick Douglass wrote in his *Autobiography*:

> I have said my master found religious sanction for his cruelty. As an example, I will state one of many facts going to prove the charge. I have seen him tie up a lame young woman, and whip her with a heavy cowskin upon her naked shoulders, causing the warm red blood to drip; and, in justification of the bloody deed, he would quote this passage of Scripture.[72]

—

> *Verily, verily, I say unto thee, Except a man be born again, he cannot see the kingdom of God.*
>
> JOHN 3:3

This is surely the signal verse of Evangelical Christianity. Ask the average American who is only nominally interested in faith and church if "born again" is in the Bible and they will be unsure; but ask an evangelical and they will point to these words of Jesus to Nicodemus. This is also the modern evangelist's most important text—from D. L. Moody, who preached again and again on this text, to Billy Graham, who wrote the book on the subject: *How to Be Born Again.*

—

> *For God so loved the world, that he gave his only begotten Son, that whosoever believeth in him should not perish, but have everlasting life.*
>
> JOHN 3:16

---

72. Douglass, *Life of Frederick Douglass*, 36.

This third chapter of John's Gospel is a treasure box for evangelical faith. R. A. Torrey, the most important student of D. L. Moody who carried on his work, famously called this "The most wonderful sentence ever written."

> *In my Father's house are many mansions: if it were not*
> *so, I would have told you.*
>
> JOHN 14:2

The KJV follows Tyndale in using this now-famous phrase, "many mansions," often used by ecumenists seeking to show that Christ was allowing for different expressions of faith. The Bishop's Bible opted for "many dwelling places."

THE ACTS OF THE APOSTLES

> *And when the day of Pentecost was fully come, they*
> *were all with one accord in one place. And suddenly*
> *there came a sound from heaven as of a rushing mighty*
> *wind, and it filled all the house where they were sitting.*
> *And there appeared unto them cloven tongues like as*
> *of fire, and it sat upon each of them. And they were*
> *all filled with the Holy Ghost, and began to speak with*
> *other tongues, as the Spirit gave them utterance.*
>
> ACTS 2:1 – 4

The KJV translators added "rushing" to Tyndale's "mighty wind" — a nice touch. But they also took the image of "cloven" (meaning simply "split") from Tyndale. You won't find "cloven" in other translations, but this one word has inspired a lot of iconology

over the years: Resting upon the heads of those present at Pente-
cost, in paintings, invariably are individual, small, hooflike flames.

———

Ananias went his way, and entered into the house; and
putting his hands on him said, Brother Saul, the Lord,
even Jesus, that appeared unto thee in the way as thou
camest, hath sent me, that thou mightest receive thy
sight, and be filled with the Holy Ghost. And immedi-
ately there fell from his eyes as it had been scales: and
he received sight forthwith, and arose, and was baptized.

ACTS 9:17–18

THE EPISTLES

I am crucified with Christ: nevertheless I live; yet not I,
but Christ liveth in me.

GALATIANS 2:20

This first half of Galatians 2:20 is one of most profound theological statements, as well as poetic expressions, in all of Scripture.
But I wonder why the KJV translators chose to remove that one
word from the Bishops' Bible version: "I am crucified with Christ.
Nevertheless, I live: yet *now* not I, but Christ liveth in me."

———

Whatsoever a man soweth, that shall he also reap.

GALATIANS 6:7

I have heard the idea from this verse quoted perhaps more than
any other idea from the Bible: You reap what you sow. People almost

universally know that this comes from the Bible, and it's most often quoted to support the idea that God has established the world with basic laws, and that violating those laws has consequences. This is the verse used to counter all of the other evidence in life that people who do wrong usually get away with it in this world just fine!

———

For we wrestle not against flesh and blood, but against principalities, against powers, against the rulers of the darkness of this world, against spiritual wickedness in high places.

EPHESIANS 6:12

No single verse has been used more often by people to describe their enemies. From the American Revolution to the struggle against Apartheid in South Africa, Christians have used these memorable phrases to depict the ways that those in power are complicit in evil of a higher (or lower) order.

———

Though I speak with the tongues of men and of angels, and have not charity, I am become as sounding brass, or a tinkling cymbal. And though I have the gift of prophecy, and understand all mysteries, and all knowledge; and though I have all faith, so that I could remove mountains, and have not charity, I am nothing. And though I bestow all my goods to feed the poor, and though I give my body to be burned, and have not charity, it profiteth me nothing. Charity suffereth long, and is kind; charity envieth not; charity vaunteth not itself, is not puffed up,

> *Doth not behave itself unseemly, seeketh not her own,*
> *is not easily provoked, thinketh no evil; Rejoiceth not in*
> *iniquity, but rejoiceth in the truth; Beareth all things, be-*
> *lieveth all things, hopeth all things, endureth all things.*
>
> 1 CORINTHIANS 13:1 – 7

I try to be realistic about the poetry of the KJV: it's not *always* the best. The most glaring instance of this stands out in the "love" chapter: 1 Corinthians 13. This is the most-quoted chapter of the Epistles of Paul. From 1 Corinthians 13, we have William Tyndale to thank, not the KJV, for architecting our modern understanding of what love means. For some reason, the KJV translators disagreed with Tyndale's use of the word, "love," here, for the Greek word that transliterates as *agape*. *Agape* means "sacrificial love." Perhaps the KJV team thought that "love" would sound too personal as a single word standing in for such an important Christian practice; or maybe they felt it would *feel* too personal. They rendered Tyndale's "Love suffereth long" as "Charity suffereth long" (v. 4), and they repeatedly rendered the Greek *agape* as "charity."

> *O death, where is thy sting? O grave, where is thy victory?*
>
> 1 CORINTHIANS 15:55

Made famous by the popular English oratorio — sung by many of us at Christmastime although it was originally written for Easter — the "Messiah," by George Frideric Handel (1685 – 1759). The libretto was written by Charles Jennens and takes much from the KJV, including this verse.

Let us draw near with a true heart in full assurance
of faith, having our hearts sprinkled from an evil con-
science, and our bodies washed with pure water.

HEBREWS 10:22

Surely one of the loveliest verses in all of Scripture, this one inspired the hymn about the atonement, "Blessed Assurance" by the blind hymn writer, Fanny Crosby (1820–1915), put to music (even more memorable than the words) by Phoebe Knapp (1839–1908). These two talented women were good friends, and both members of John Street Methodist Episcopal Church in New York City.

The word of the Lord endureth for ever.

1 PETER 1:25

As the Church of England became increasingly identified with Protestantism over the course of the century leading up to the KJV, this verse was often quoted and took on new meaning, as an expression for how the Word of God had dethroned the pope.

Clouds they are without water, carried about of winds;
trees whose fruit withereth, without fruit, twice dead,
plucked up by the roots; Raging waves of the sea, foam-
ing out their own shame; wandering stars, to whom is
reserved the blackness of darkness for ever.

JUDE 12–13

These memorable, poetic phrasings are all describing false teachers in the early Christian communities. Notably, "wandering stars" was the phrase often used by ancient and medieval people for what we call the "naked-eye planets," or those planets that can be seen without a telescope (Mercury, Venus, Mars, Jupiter, and Saturn). Ancient Judaism added the Sun and the Moon and made it the "seven heavenly objects" that, according to Josephus (37–c. 100 CE), gave rise to the seven branches of the Jewish Menorah.

REVELATION

To him that overcometh will I give to eat of the hidden manna, and will give him a white stone, and in the stone a new name written, which no man knoweth saving he that receiveth it.

REVELATION 2:17

The message of this verse is close to the heart of contemplative Christians around the world. It has inspired many monastics over the centuries, as it speaks poignantly to the personal relationship that God has with each person, so personal that when we become intimate friends with God, we may come so close as to know him in ways that hint at a different name for ourselves that we don't yet know, that only God knows and will reveal to us in due time.

———

Behold, I stand at the door, and knock: if any man hear my voice, and open the door, I will come in to him, and will sup with him, and he with me.

REVELATION 3:20

———

> And I looked, and behold a white cloud, and upon the
> cloud one sat like unto the Son of man, having on his
> head a golden crown, and in his hand a sharp sickle. And
> another angel came out of the temple, crying with a loud
> voice to him that sat on the cloud, Thrust in thy sickle,
> and reap: for the time is come for thee to reap; for the
> harvest of the earth is ripe. And he that sat on the cloud
> thrust in his sickle on the earth; and the earth was reaped.
>
> REVELATION 14:14–16

—

This passage is rich in connotations that have been plumbed in literature and popular culture over the centuries — the apocalyptic vision of Jesus Christ as a reaper at the end of time.

> [T]he angel thrust in his sickle into the earth, and gathered
> the vine of the earth, and cast it into the great winepress
> of the wrath of God. And the winepress was trodden
> without the city, and blood came out of the winepress,
> even unto the horse bridles, by the space of a thousand
> and six hundred furlongs.
>
> REVELATION 14:19-20

Together with Genesis 3:15 (bruising the head of the serpent), Isaiah 66:1 (the earth as God's footstool), and Revelation 16:14 ("the battle of that great day of God Almighty"), this passage inspired the imagery for the most famous of songs of the American Civil War, "Battle Hymn of the Republic" (lyrics by Julian Ward Howe, 1861). Revelation 14:19's "great winepress of the wrath of God" became "the grapes of wrath" of the song — and subsequently, of John Steinbeck's famous novel by the same name (published in 1939).

PROVERBS FROM THE GOOD BOOK

The grass withereth, the flower fadeth:
but the word of our God shall stand for ever.

ISAIAH 40:8

If you've ever memorized verses of the Bible, you know how they can later pop to mind at the most unexpected moments. Someone once said, "For what is small and well-put sticks in the heart."[73] That's just right, and the KJV is well-suited.

A good proverb speaks in the present imperative — causing us to sit up and take notice. *Bartlett's Familiar Quotations* includes entire sections of proverbs from the KJV, and not only from the Book of Proverbs. The King James Bible is, from cover to cover, a treasure trove of practical and earthy wisdom.

Billy Graham, the great American evangelist, had a daily devotional practice that involved reading five psalms and then one of the thirty-one chapters of Proverbs. He often said that the psalms "teach me how to get along with God," and the proverbs, "teach me how to get along with others."

---

73. J. M. Cohen, ed., trans. *The Penguin Book of Spanish Verse* (New York: Penguin, 1965), 14.

The proverbs found in the King James Bible sound like what your grandmother or grandfather used to tell you—like the wisdom of a bygone age. The images and metaphors grab us by the shoulders and shake sense into us. As Proverbs 19:8 summarizes it,

> *He that getteth wisdom loveth his own soul:*
> *he that keepeth understanding shall find good.*

Here is a thematic list of some proverb favorites.

AUTHENTICITY

Dead flies cause the ointment of the apothecary to send forth a stinking savor.

ECCLESIASTES 10:1

DISCIPLINE

The sluggard will not plow by reason of the cold; therefore shall he beg in harvest, and have nothing.

PROVERBS 20:4

FAITHFULNESS

Rejoice, O young man, in thy youth; and let thy heart cheer thee in the days of thy youth, and walk in the ways of thine heart, and in the sight of thine eyes: but know thou, that for all these things God will bring thee into judgment. Therefore remove sorrow from thy heart, and put away evil from thy flesh: for childhood

*and youth are vanity. Remember now thy Creator in
the days of thy youth.*

ECCLESIASTES 11:9 – 10, 12:1

FAMILY

*Honor thy father and thy mother: that thy days may be
long upon the land which the LORD thy God giveth thee.*

EXODUS 20:12

*It is better to dwell in the wilderness than with a conten-
tios and an angry woman.*

PROVERBS 21:19

FRIENDS

Depart from evil, and do good; seek peace, and pursue it.

PSALM 34:14

*The fruit of the righteous is a tree of life; and he that win-
neth souls is wise.*

PROVERBS 11:30

*He that walketh with wise men shall be wise: but a com-
panion of fools shall be destroyed.*

PROVERBS 13:20

GIVING

*When thou doest alms, let not thy left hand know what
thy right hand doeth: That thine alms may be in secret:*

and thy Father which seeth in secret himself shall reward
thee openly.

MATTHEW 6:3 – 4

HEART

The heart is deceitful above all things, and desperately
wicked: who can know it? I the LORD search the heart,
I try the reins, even to give every man according to his
ways, and according to the fruit of his doings.

JEREMIAH 17:9 – 10

Who shall ascend into the hill of the LORD? or who shall
stand in his holy place? He that hath clean hands, and a
pure heart.

PSALM 24:3 – 4

HONESTY

Every way of a man is right in his own eyes: but the
LORD pondereth the hearts.

PROVERBS 21:2

My lips shall not speak wickedness, nor my tongue utter
deceit.

JOB 27:4

HOPE

Hope deferred maketh the heart sick: but when the
desire cometh, it is a tree of life.

PROVERBS 13:12

*He that ... weepeth ... shall doubtless come again ...
rejoicing.*

PSALM 126:6

HOSPITALITY

*Better is a dinner of herbs where love is, than a stalled
ox and hatred therewith.*

PROVERBS 15:17

*Verily I say unto you, Inasmuch as ye have done it unto
one of the least of these my brethren, ye have done it
unto me.*

MATTHEW 25:40

KNOWLEDGE

*Every prudent man dealeth with knowledge: but a fool
layeth open his folly.*

PROVERBS 13:16

Thus saith the LORD, *Let not the wise man glory in his
wisdom, neither let the mighty man glory in his might,
let not the rich man glory in his riches: But let him
that glorieth glory in this, that he understandeth and
knoweth me.*

JEREMIAH 9:23 – 24

*Cease, my son, to hear the instruction that causeth to err
from the words of knowledge.*

PROVERBS 19:27

LISTENING

*A fool uttereth all his mind: but a wise man keepeth it
in till afterwards.*

PROVERBS 29:11

*Even a fool, when he holdeth his peace, is counted wise:
and he that shutteth his lips is esteemed a man of understanding.*

PROVERBS 17:28

LOVE

*Greater love hath no man than this, that a man lay
down his life for his friends.*

JOHN 15:13

*There is no fear in love; but perfect love casteth out fear:
because fear hath torment. He that feareth is not made
perfect in love.*

1 JOHN 4:18

MARRIAGE

Rejoice with the wife of thy youth.

PROVERBS 5:18

OPTIMISM

*A merry heart doeth good like a medicine: but a broken
spirit drieth the bones.*

PROVERBS 17:22

PASSION

*Thou shalt love the LORD thy God with all thine heart,
and with all thy soul, and with all thy might.*

DEUTERONOMY 6:5

PATIENCE

*To every thing there is a season, and a time to every
purpose under the heaven.*

ECCLESIASTES 3:1

*The preparations of the heart in man, and the answer of
the tongue, is from the LORD.*

PROVERBS 16:1

*God will not cast away a perfect man. . . . Till he fill thy
mouth with laughing, and thy lips with rejoicing.*

JOB 8:20–21

POSSESSIONS

*Lay not up for yourselves treasures upon earth, where
moth and rust doth corrupt, and where thieves break
through and steal: But lay up for yourselves treasures in
heaven, where neither moth nor rust doth corrupt, and
where thieves do not break through nor steal.*

MATTHEW 6:19–20

PRIDE

Pride goeth before destruction, and an haughty spirit before a fall.

PROVERBS 16:18

RESPECT

The fear of the LORD is the beginning of wisdom: and the knowledge of the holy is understanding.

PROVERBS 9:10

SADNESS

Sorrow is better than laughter: for by the sadness of the countenance the heart is made better.

ECCLESIASTES 7:3

SPEECH

A wholesome tongue is a tree of life: but perverseness therein is a breach in the spirit.

PROVERBS 15:4

TELLING THE TRUTH

He that covereth his sins shall not prosper: but whoso confesseth and forsaketh them shall have mercy.

PROVERBS 28:13

TRUST

Thus saith the LORD; *Cursed be the man that trusteth
in man, and maketh flesh his arm, and whose heart
departeth from the* LORD. *For he shall be like the heath
in the desert, and shall not see when good cometh; but
shall inhabit the parched places in the wilderness, in
a salt land and not inhabited. Blessed is the man that
trusteth in the* LORD, *and whose hope the* LORD *is. For
he shall be as a tree planted by the waters, and that
spreadeth out her roots by the river, and shall not see
when heat cometh, but her leaf shall be green; and shall
not be careful in the year of drought, neither shall cease
from yielding fruit.*

JEREMIAH 17:5 – 8

WEALTH

*As the partridge sitteth on eggs, and hatcheth them not;
so he that getteth riches, and not by right, shall leave
them in the midst of his days, and at his end shall be a
fool.*

JEREMIAH 17:11

*Wealth gotten by vanity shall be diminished: but he that
gathereth by labor shall increase.*

PROVERBS 13:11

Where your treasure is, there will your heart be also.

MATTHEW 6:21

WISDOM

A wise man feareth, and departeth from evil: but the fool rageth, and is confident.

PROVERBS 14:16

It is an honor for a man to cease from strife: but every fool will be meddling.

PROVERBS 20:3

It is as sport to a fool to do mischief: but a man of understanding hath wisdom.

PROVERBS 10:23

The wise shall inherit glory: but shame shall be the promotion of fools.

PROVERBS 3:35

A wise man is strong; yea, a man of knowledge increaseth strength.

PROVERBS 24:5

He that getteth wisdom loveth his own soul: he that keepeth understanding shall find good.

PROVERBS 19:8

Behold, I send you forth as sheep in the midst of wolves: be ye therefore wise as serpents, and harmless as doves.

MATTHEW 10:16

The heart of the righteous studieth to answer: but the mouth of the wicked poureth out evil things.

PROVERBS 15:28

WORK

He that gathereth in summer is a wise son: but he that sleepeth in harvest is a son that causeth shame.

PROVERBS 10:5

Go to the ant, thou sluggard; consider her ways, and be wise.

PROVERBS 6:6

WORRIES

Take therefore no thought for the morrow: for the morrow shall take thought for the things of itself. Sufficient unto the day is the evil thereof.

MATTHEW 6:34

YOUTH

Those that seek me early shall find me.

PROVERBS 8:17

THE BIBLE
AND WONDER

Praise ye the Lord.

REPEATED REFRAIN, PSALMS 146–50

Ye men of Galilee, why stand ye gazing up into heaven?

ACTS 1:11

On January 15, 1996, the universe grew by forty billion galaxies."[74] The Hubble Space Telescope was sending back pictures of what we used to call "the heavens," and it was on that day that it took a picture that vastly expanded the vision of our place in the world. This is part of why so many of the images of the KJV feel unusual to us moderns: we've learned to see galaxies far beyond our own, and our imagination for what is *unknown* has shrunk just about as far.

While the KJV era was not entirely pre-science (Copernicus predates it by a century, for instance), for the most part, the universe was a place of unknowns in 1611. At that point in history,

---

74. Richard Panek, *Seeing and Believing: How the Telescope Opened Our Eyes and Minds to the Heavens* (New York: Viking, 1998), 1.

exploration was becoming more common; people were growing more interested in discovering what lies beyond them; and they easily accepted the fact that the Bible spoke about a lot of inexplicable things.

While the KJV translation committees were finishing their deliberations, Galileo aimed his first telescope at the skies from Padua, Italy. He soon made his first statements about the organization of the heavens and the earth, telling friends and colleagues that Copernicus was right and the Sacred Scriptures were ... not wrong exactly ... but misused and misunderstood. Images such as an immovable earth or God's "hands" and "eyes" were devices, he argued, that made sense to the first men and women who read and heard them and were intended to motivate believers toward greater devotion and faithfulness.

The worldview of the premodern seventeenth century was vastly different from our own. Four hundred years of scientific discoveries, globalization, secularism, and the Enlightenment have led us to see things differently.

Seventeenth-century people perceived much less difference between the "real" world and the world of the Bible. The two were mostly one and the same. Their earthly world was linked to the spirit world, and spirits and angelic beings were commonly understood to be moving back and forth between the two realms. When Christians prayed the Sanctus during worship (just as many of us who are in liturgical traditions still do)—"Holy, holy, holy Lord, / God of power and might ..."—they could more easily "see" the angels they were joining when they intoned these ancient words (specifically, from Isaiah 6:3).

The fact is, the language of the KJV helped Christians to "see" what we see less of today—things like the soul, the afterlife, heaven, even sin, and the ordinary ways that people once envisioned God: in the clouds, in a military victory, in the sunrise, as a baby lying in a cow's feeding trough, or as a shepherd who cares for his sheep.

Does this mean that the KJV is less valuable to us today? (I've noticed that there doesn't seem to be much in-between.)

There are many who say yes, it is less relevant. Many translators today insist that the old images and metaphors in the KJV should be discarded, or else, how are we to really understand what the text is trying to say? For example, translation theory today suggests that for a word such as the one for "shepherd," *ro'eh*, as it is transliterated in Hebrew, we find an English equivalent that makes more sense in our culture and experience. If you have lived your life in the West and Global North, when was the last time that you actually saw a shepherd? Do you know what shepherds really do? Probably not. That's the point, as one translator suggests: "Our first warning sign that something has gone wrong in the translation is that a common, familiar word like *ro'eh* has been translated as a rare, unfamiliar one. While '*ro'eh*' was common in Hebrew, 'shepherd' is uncommon in English. We know that this is always a mistake."[75]

Really? I cannot understand something profound about the Lord in Psalm 23 through the image of a shepherd? This particular translator—one of today's best from Hebrew to English—goes on to suggest that English words such as *Marine, fireman, lawyer, cowboy, lumberjack,* and *farmer* would all be better than sticking with *shepherd.*[76] Let it never be so! I believe that the very strangeness, slight foreignness, of the KJV—much more pronounced today than

---

75. Joel M. Hoffman, *And God Said: How Translations Conceal the Bible's Original Meaning* (New York: Thomas Dunne, 2010), 129.

76. Ibid., 133–35.

it was in the seventeenth century—is precisely what sometimes makes reading the Bible meaningful, beautiful, and memorable.

Does this mean that a *shepherd* needs to become a *protector* or some sort of strong man? Should the baby Jesus have been born in a portable crib instead of a manger?

Instead, I like the ways that the KJV can fill an imagination. This is because, ultimately, I believe, with Moses, that I am "a stranger in a strange land" (Exodus 2:22).

To a sixteenth- or seventeenth-century person, the third person of the Trinity—the Holy Ghost—was easy to imagine. What had been *Spiritus* in the Vulgate's Latin, most often became *Ghost* in Tyndale and in the KJV—and then has become *Spirit* again in the modern era. Perhaps we think that *Ghost* is too visible to convey what *Spirit* more properly keeps invisible? *Ghost* versus *Spirit* is just one example of some of the ways that the modern worldview lost something tangible, fascinating, and compelling in ways that only some of the most clever and imaginative writers have reclaimed today.

Other spiritual beings were captured in the phrases of the KJV. For example, Hebrews 13:2 framed the ancient, mystical purpose of hospitality like this:

> Be not forgetful to entertain strangers: for thereby some
> have entertained angels unawares.

I find that rendering so much more vivid than more recent translations! Can't you just imagine *angels unawares*? Certainly more than you can imagine this: "Do not neglect to show hospitality to strangers, for by doing that some have entertained angels without knowing it" (NRSV). Which version is more likely to grab the generation that has grown up on Harry Potter?

SOME FAIRLY FANTASTIC CREATURES

If you have begun to read the KJV for the first time, you've probably been surprised to discover that it contains some fantastic creatures. The lost world of the KJV imagines little distinction between what is real and what may be imagined. Their worldview included many possibilities; their senses taught them that the as-yet-unknown was as real as what had been clearly verified; it was easier for them to believe than not to believe.

They embraced the mythological. For example, the KJV describes a universe that includes creatures like satyrs (half man, half goat), and its description of what happens in a bad place is almost beyond imagination. Check out Isaiah 13:

> *And Babylon, the glory of kingdoms, the beauty of the Chaldees' excellency, shall be as when God overthrew Sodom and Gomorrah.... But wild beasts of the desert shall lie there; and their houses shall be full of doleful creatures; and owls shall dwell there, and satyrs shall dance there.*
>
> 19, 21

A satyr was firmly established as a folkloric creature from Greek and Roman mythology centuries earlier. The Hebrew word that the KJV translates "satyr," is *se'irim*, which means "hairy ones," usually a kind of demon. Our translators definitely wanted to retain the mythical feeling of this passage—in which, in most modern translations, *satyrs* become simply "wild goats." *Se'irim* is elsewhere rendered as "devils" by the KJV (Leviticus 17:7).

The KJV is also home to cockatrices, a sort of rooster-serpent that can kill other creatures in a flash. No one ever lived to tell of seeing one, since to glimpse it was to die instantly. As Juliet says in

Romeo and Juliet: "I shall poison more / Than the death-darting eye of cockatrice." This mythical creature, strangely, plays a part in the vision of the "Peaceable Kingdom"—the prophet Isaiah's vision of an idyllic future ruled by gentleness, justice, and the righteousness of the Messiah—when there will be no danger and no death: "And the sucking child shall play on the hole of the asp, and the weaned child shall put his hand on the cockatrice's den. They shall not hurt nor destroy in all my holy mountain" (Isaiah 11:8–9). Not a snake's den or an adder's den or a viper's den, but a creature more dangerous and certainly more uncertain.

There's more. There's a race of giants that somehow survived Noah's Flood. And Numbers 23:22 compares God's strength to that of a unicorn: "God brought them out of Egypt; he hath as it were the strength of an unicorn." In the Book of Job, God describes a beast that the KJV calls a "behemoth." Some creationists refer to this passage as evidence that this behemoth was a dinosaur:

> *Behold now behemoth, which I made with thee; he eateth grass as an ox. Lo now, his strength is in his loins, and his force is in the navel of his belly. He moveth his tail like a cedar: the sinews of his stones are wrapped together.*
>
> JOB 40:15–17

Behemoth has actually been retained by most translations ever since, both Jewish and Christian, including the NRSV. The behemoth is thought by noncreationists to be a sort of primal monster, an example of a great mythic beast. Its parallel in the water is the leviathan, also mentioned a few times in the KJV and also repeated in other translations:

> *In that day the LORD with his sore and great and strong sword shall punish leviathan the piercing serpent, even le-*

> *viathan that crooked serpent; and he shall slay the dragon*
> *that is in the sea.*
>
> ISAIAH 27:1

The list of mythical creatures goes on. These things are pre-sented as if they are as real as the animals we know today. To the people of a bygone age, these fantastic creatures were as real as the fish in Peter's nets — demonstrations of how they imagined things that don't actually exist in order to explain some of life's uncertainties.

You could say that including such things in the KJV is a sign that the translators made mistakes in judgment. The *unicorn* in Numbers becomes a *wild ox* in the NRSV; the *satyrs* in Isaiah 13 become *goat-demons*; and the *cockatrice* of Isaiah 11 becomes a *viper* in the NIV.

The race of giants in Genesis is something else. This is a case where translators have always had to make educated guesses as to what the words of the original languages mean. Genesis 6:4 begins, "There were giants in the earth in those days ...," describing a tribe of people that were present before Noah's Flood (and also providing the title of O. E. Rolvaag's classic novel of prairie life, *Giants in the Earth*). The Greek word from the Septuagint is *gigantes*, meaning literally "born of the earth." The Hebrew word from the Torah is *nephilim*. No one really knows what *nephilim* meant then — or might mean now. The root word, *nephel*, means "unfortunate birth." The NRSV and other translations have simply retained *nephilim* to describe these mystery men from ancient times.

Even if these are invented stories and imaginary creatures, they are part of what once created a people. They were a way of speaking to the fears, quandaries, and anxieties of life. But does this mean that we, today, should fear coming across a cockatrice in the woods or a satyr when we go out dancing? What's a modern to do with all of this?

WONDER VS. IMAGINATION

When my kids were little, I wanted them to have a sense of wonder and a vivid imagination. I read them the Brothers Grimm and Mother Goose, and I regaled them with tales of a jolly fat man who brings presents to boys and girls on Christmas Eve.

I even encouraged my kids to believe in fairies.

We lived in a log cabin in the woods, and on walks I would tell the kids that fairies lived there, and that they watched over us, just like angels do. Over the course of one summer when my kids were still quite young, one of them wrote frequent notes to the fairies, placing them in the trees to discover at night, and I would surreptitiously fetch the notes and write back in my own sort of fairy script.

One evening a year or two after the fairy correspondence had ended, we were having dinner at a nice restaurant in late November. We got talking about Christmas. By this point in time, I imagined that the kids had begun to hear from their more jaded friends at school that Santa Claus was a myth. So when my daughter said, "Santa really *does* exist, doesn't he?" I froze. *Should I come clean, finally?* I wondered.

"Well ... actually ... Santa isn't really true," I said, "but he's a fun part of Christmas, I think," rising at the last, trying to give hope just as I was dashing it.

"What?" my daughter yelled, crestfallen and already in tears.

Then she burst out with, "What *else* have you been lying about!?"

I had to fess up completely. The Easter Bunny. The Tooth Fairy. Even the fairies in the woods. All of them—dead.

I had created a fantasy for my kids that was ultimately unable to match reality. I helped to inspire their imaginations, but I cultivated in them a love for what *I* knew wasn't true. I should have inspired them as the King James Bible has inspired me: to imagine the reality of unseen things that I already know from my own life to be *true*.

LIVING IN WONDER

Child psychologist Bruno Bettelheim once said:

> As long as parents fully believed that Biblical stories solved the riddle of our existence and its purpose, it was easy to make a child feel secure. The Bible was felt to contain the answers to all pressing questions: the Bible told man all he needed to know to understand the world, how it came into being, and how to behave in it. In the Western world the Bible also provided prototypes for man's imagination.[77]

I suspect that this is true. I certainly had that feeling of security when I was a child.

Wonder expands us and feeds our hope. Wonder isn't an activity. You'd never say to a guest, "Pardon me for a few minutes while I walk outside in the garden and wonder." Rather, wonder is a capacity that grows, and will grow, given the right encouragement and environment. It's a capacity we are born with, and I think it is helped along by the power of the Holy Spirit.

---

77. Bruno Bettelheim, *The Uses of Enchantment: The Meaning and Importance of Fairy Tales*; New York: Vintage Books, 1989; 52.

When I was a child, my capacity for wonder was grown by the language of our church and the King James Bible. The language formed me forever. I was a child raised to understand God as an intimate friend — so intimate that he lives *in* me — and this has influenced my understandings and aspirations. Angels had charge over me, watching my step, and I was kind to strangers because they may have been angels unawares. I also learned that this intimacy included certain spiritual feelings and experiences, not all of them clear; the Lord was my shepherd; he led me beside still waters, and sometimes, he made me lie down in green pastures; when I was scared, his rod and staff comforted me.

A NEW AND OLD LANGUAGE

The English that we speak at work or the dinner table is often the same English we speak at church. It wasn't always so, however. The KJV offers a language that is slightly outside of everyday experience, which expands our capacity to contemplate, see, and know God. Before the modern era, when translations became more abundant, Christian English-speakers were basically bilingual — everyday English and KJV English existed side-by-side.

What I am proposing is a rediscovery and reinvigoration of this sort of English bilingualism. Reading a Bible that's a little bit difficult, and unusual, is *good* for you.

Many Christians today feel vaguely homesick, like people in exile. History has taken us far from our linguistic home, and we long to return there. We long to hear the rhythms of the King James Bible once again, the rhythms that call us back to a place where we can stand in the dark beneath the canopy of the heavens and gaze into the unknown.

When this happens—when we begin to discover or rediscover the King James Bible—our hearts and minds and imaginations begin to expand. I think back to more than a year ago when I decided to begin reading from page 1 in my newly purchased KJV. Genesis chapter 1, verse 1, "In the beginning God." I hadn't read through the Bible since my days in high school youth group.

That first day, a flood of nostalgia overcame me. I found myself remembering strange long-ago things like flannel-board lessons from Sunday school and vacation-Bible-school themes on the Creation. As one who knew the KJV in childhood, I quickly had doubts. Was I wasting my time?

But as I read on, day after day, ten pages each day, I found myself immersed in the stories and language and imagination of the King James Version. Oh, the places I traveled! On Day One alone, I walked in the Garden of Eden in the cool of the day and heard the voice of the Lord. As I read, I found that I was paying attention to the words of the Bible more than I had for many years. The strangeness of words arrested me. The odd verb endings caused me to trip from time to time—and then I found that I stubbornly wanted to plumb deeper and understand everything more fully.

Above all, I began to wonder and imagine in the words of the Bible once again. I found myself listening for God's voice, and hearing it in different ways and in new places.

May you do the same.

Four hundred years have passed since this landmark book first appeared. It's the most important book ever published. May you give it a chance to work wonders in your own life.

The 1611 translators said many things exceedingly well. May this be our benediction:

It remaineth that we commend thee to God, and to the Spirit of his grace, which is able to build further than we can ask or think. He removeth the scales from our eyes, the veil from our hearts, opening our wits that we may understand his word, enlarging our hearts, yea, correcting our affections, that we may love it above gold and silver, yea, that we may love it to the end. Amen.[78]

---

78. This word occurs seventy-six times in the KJV (not as many times as I guessed, before looking it up), beginning in Numbers 5:22 in a very strange verse (check it out) that ends with "Amen, amen," and lastly with the beautiful benediction of Revelation 22:21, "The grace of our Lord Jesus Christ be with you all. Amen."

Appendix

A QUICK GUIDE TO ARCHAIC WORDS AND PHRASES

Every word of God is pure.

Proverbs 30:5

The KJV translators explained in their preface that they were motivated to use a variety of English words to express what was said in the original languages. They had flair and insisted that a beautiful bouquet must include a variety of flowers: "For is the kingdom of God become words or syllables? Why should we be in bondage to them, if we may be free?"

There is no question that the KJV is full of words and phrases that puzzle us today. Some of the translators' choices no longer communicate effectively. Consider, for instance, this single verse from Judges 16:15:

> *And she said unto him, How canst thou say, I love thee, when thine heart is not with me? thou hast mocked me these three times, and hast not told me wherein thy great strength lieth.*

No one would blame you for responding, *Hmm . . . what?* Those archaic verb and pronoun forms can be confusing to say the least.

Also, the meanings of words simply evolve over time. A *storyteller* was something like a gossip, in the seventeenth century. To be *sturdy* was usually to be not just large, but brutal. To be *brilliant* was only for the lustrous, like a diamond. Similarly, biblical words have evolved over the centuries, and many of the words in the KJV have long ago been changed to more contemporary equivalents in modern translations. For example, if you want to be really confused, check out, below, the archaic meaning that the KJV uses for the verb *let*.

For those of us who still want to read the classic Authorized Version, here is a brief guide to some of the more common ones. Proper nouns are left out, since there are enough proper nouns starting with K and Z, alone, to fill many pages! (*Kerioth*, a town in south Judah and a city in Moab; *Kezia*, Job's second daughter; *Korhites*, a priestly family related to the Levites; *Ziph*, a son of Jehaleleel as well as a city in the mountains of Judah; and on and on; okay!). And verbs are discussed at the bottom of the list.

affections (pl. n.)—passion, and, contrary to our modern understanding, it's not necessarily positive. It appears twice in the New Testament: Romans 1:26, where it's preceded by the adjective *vile*; and Galatians 5:24, where it's joined with *lusts*.

afore (adv.)—before

aforesaid (adj.)—spoken of earlier

aforetime (adv.)—in times past; formerly

ague (n.)—a fever or chill. Appears only once, in Leviticus 26:16.

alas (interj.)—an exclamation of sorrow or grief, as in "And when

Gideon perceived that he was an angel of the LORD, Gideon said, Alas, O Lord God! for because I have seen an angel of the LORD face to face" (Judges 6:22). Sometimes repeated twice, as in "Alas, alas."

albeit (conj.) — shortened version of "although it be that"

ambassage (n.) — used only once, in Luke 14:32, meaning "embassy" or "ambassadors"

amen (interj. and n.) — an affirmation of having trust and confidence; "so be it" or "it is true"; curiously, it is at least once used as a noun, as in "All the promises of God in [Christ] are yea, and in him Amen" (2 Corinthians 1:20).

astonied (adj.) — an archaic adjective with a meaning equivalent to our word *astonished*. See Isaiah 52:14. (Repeated later in the Revised Version)

behold (v.) — look!

betimes (adv.) — soon, or in good time

bewray (v.) — reveal or betray

blain (n.) — a blotch or blister, as in the sixth plague in Egypt, sometimes known as "the boils and the blains" (Exodus 9:9) plague

bruit (n.) — rumor. See Jeremiah 10:22 and Nahum 3:19.

buckler (n.) — this word occurs eleven times in the Old Testament, never in the New, it usually means "shield," although the KJV mistakenly uses it to mean "spear" in 1 Chronicles 12:8.

bullock (n.) — cow or ox

by and by (adv.) — straightway, soon

caul (n.) — a membrane in a mammal's abdomen, followed by the phrase "above the liver" in eleven instances in the Old Testament

chaff (n.) — the husk that is separated from the corn or grain; used as a metaphor for something without use or worth, as in Luke

3:17

clave (v.) — the past tense of *cleave*. Can mean "adhere," as in "Certain men clave unto him and believed" (Acts 17:34), or "split," as in "he clave the rock also, and the waters gushed out" (Isaiah 48:21).

cockatrice (n.) — like a dragon, this is a creature of ancient legend, believed to be a poisonous serpent that was born from a rooster egg

conversation (n.) — means a variety of things, and often not just talking. In "For our conversation is in heaven," it means "fellowship." In exhortations toward "holy conversation and godliness" (2 Peter 3:11) and "be ye holy in all manner of conversation" (1 Peter 1:15) it means virtue of all kinds. Still, it can have negative connotations, as in 2 Peter 2:8: "... vexed with the filthy conversations of the wicked."

cornet (n.) — trumpet

dainty (n.) — delicious food, as in this warning from Solomon: "When thou sittest to eat with a ruler, consider diligently what is before thee.... Be not desirous of his dainties: for they are deceitful meat" (Proverbs 23:1, 3)

dayspring (n.) — dawn, or rising sun. Sadly, this bit of poetry is rarely used today. See Job 38:12 and Luke 1:78.

diadem (n.) — crown or tiara

divers (adj.) — different, various

doom (n.) — judgment. Only one instance, from the Apocrypha: "But the day of doom shall be the end of this time, and the beginning of the immortality for to come" (2 Esdras 7:43)

dross (n.) — impurities separated from silver when it is melted down

emerods (n.) — hemorrhoids; occurs eight times in the Old Testament, seven times in two chapters of 1 Samuel and then this verse (from a list of curses), which reminds me of how we used to laugh about it in Sunday school! "The Lord will smite thee with the botch of Egypt, and with the emerods, and with the scab, and with the itch, whereof thou canst not be healed" (28:27).

ensign (n.)—this word has a few different meanings: a sign used by a tribe, a banner used by an army, and a flag or other visible signal

eschew (v.)—to avoid, or run from

faint (v.)—to grow weary or give up, as in Luke 18:1 where it says "men ought always to pray, and not to faint"

fallow (adj. or n.)—inactive, or ground left uncultivated

fodder (n.)—livestock feed, or mixture

forasmuch (adv.)—akin to our words *since*, *because*, or *seeing*, and always followed by *as* or *that* to demonstrate a connection between two ideas or things

forthwith (adv.)—right away

fuller's field (n.)—a place on the near-west side of Jerusalem where fullers (cloth-makers) made their living; see 2 Kings 18:17

gall (n.)—a bitter herbal vinegar, as during Christ's crucifixion: "They gave him vinegar to drink mingled with gall" (Matthew 27:34)

gay (adj.)—different from modern usage, means "expensive" in the KJV. Used once in the New Testament and once in the Apocrypha. See James 2:3.

glass (n.)—sometimes used to mean "mirror"—a usage still common in British English. Remember how A. A. Milne describes Winnie-the-Pooh "doing his Stoutness Exercises in front of the glass." The word occurs eight times in the New Testament, five times for what we today call "glass," and three times for what

we today call "mirror." For the former, see 1 Corinthians 13:12,
"For now we see through a glass, darkly."

graven, graving (v., n.)—sculpted or carved; artistic work

habitation (n.)—place or state of dwelling. This word appears
eighty-five times in the original KJV, as in "The Lord ... bless-
eth the habitation of the just" (Proverbs 3:33).

hale (v.)—to pull, drag, like today's word *haul*. See Luke 12:58.

hallow (v.)—to treat as sacred

hart (n.)—a male deer; occurs eleven times in the KJV, but most-
often quoted from Psalm 42:1, "As the hart panteth after the
water brooks, so panteth my soul after thee, O God"

hireling (n.)—employed laborer

holpen (v.)—the antiquated past participle of *help*, as in "He
that is holpen shall fall down" (Isaiah 31:3), and in the Virgin
Mary's famous Magnificat: "He hath holpen his servant Israel,
in remembrance of his mercy; As he spake to our fathers, to
Abraham, and to his seed for ever" (Luke 1:54–55).

husbandman (n.)—farmer, tiller of the soil. See John 15:1, "I am
the true vine, and my Father is the husbandman."

inasmuch (less common) *and* **insomuch** (more common; both
adv.)—roughly translate to "because" or "to such a degree"
and are followed by either *as* or *that*. The most famous instance
comes from the words of Christ in Matthew 25:40: "And the
King shall answer and say unto them, Verily I say unto you,
Inasmuch as ye have done it unto one of the least of these my
brethren, ye have done it unto me."

inkhorn (n.)—this word appears three times in the KJV, all in
one passage of Ezekiel 9. It means a cup used for holding ink,
attached to the girdle of a writer.

jasper (n.)—an opaque mineral like quartz

jot (n. or v.)—not so unfamiliar, we inherited this bit of slang from

New Testament Greek. As a noun, *jot* (from the Greek *iota*) is the smallest letter in the Greek alphabet, and the KJV saw no need to translate such a word in this verse from Matthew: "For verily I say unto you, Till heaven and earth pass, one jot or one tittle shall in no wise pass from the law, till all be fulfilled" (5:18). A *tittle*, by the way, is a diacritical mark in any sort of writing (like the dot at the top of the letter *j*).

kick (v.) — to spurn. See 1 Samuel 2:29.

kine (n.) — buffalo. As in Pharaoh's dream, "And, behold, there came up out of the river seven kine, fatfleshed and well favored" (Genesis 41:18).

know (v.) — often means "to have sexual relations with." As in "And Adam knew Eve his wife" (Genesis 4:1).

latchet (n.) — a sandal strap

leasing (v.) — falsehood, as in "O ye sons of men, how long will ye turn my glory into shame? how long will ye love vanity, and seek after leasing?" (Psalm 4:2)

let (v.) — sometimes meaning "hinder" rather than "allow." As when God says, "I will work, and who shall let it?" (Isaiah 43:13).

list (v.) — to incline or choose, as in "The wind bloweth where it listeth" (John 3:8)

lo (interj.) — usually with an exclamation mark following it, *Lo!* is similar to *See!* or the French *Voilà!*

lucre (n.) — profits; financial gain

mammon (n.) — wealth

mantle (n.) — a splendid robe

mean (adj.) — humble, as in "the mean man boweth down" (Isaiah 2:9)

meanest (v.) — intend, or to "have in mind." This is an example of the –st verb ending (see the section on "Archaic Verb Forms" below for more detail), which is used in conjunction with the second person singular pronoun, *thou*, as in Genesis 33:8, "What meanest thou by all this ...?" Or the shipmaster to Jonah: "What meanest thou, O sleeper?" (1:6)

meat (n.) — sometimes means "wheat" or food sustenance gotten from grain, instead of animal flesh. When it means the latter, the word usually follows *savory* or precedes *offering*; for the former meaning, see Genesis 1:29 in the Garden of Eden.

meet (adj.) — fitting or proper, as in "It was meet that we should make merry" (Luke 15:32). Many wedding ceremonies use the odd word *helpmate*, a corruption of *helpmeet* ("I will make him an help meet for him" Genesis 2:18). But *meet* means "suitable," not "mate"!

murrain (n.) — an infectious disease in livestock, as in the fifth plague in Egypt, which is described as "a very grievous murrain" (Exodus 9:3)

napkin (n.) — cloth

necromancer (n.) — one who speaks with the dead

nether (adj.) — lower or below, most memorably occurring five times in Ezekiel chapters 31–32 referring to "the nether parts of the earth"

nitre (n.) — a substance that came from the bottom of a lake, named after Lake Natron in Egypt, similar to bicarbonate of soda. See Proverbs 25:20 and Jeremiah 2:22.

organ (n.) — another word the meaning of which the Hebrew seems to have escaped the KJV translators. It should've been translated "flute," as in the description of Jubal's descendants being known in ancient Israel for playing ... *the organ!* "And his brother's name was Jubal: he was the father of all such as handle the harp and organ" (Genesis 4:21). The NIV properly has it as "harp and flute." The NRSV has it as "lyre and pipe."

ouch (n.)—this word came directly from the Old English; it occurs twenty-eight times, all in Exodus, when the writer is describing the elaborate garments being designed for Aaron. Ouches were sockets in which gems or gold were set.

outlandish (adj.)—doesn't quite mean "strange" as we use the word today, but "alien" or "from a foreign country"; this meaning still survives in Southern mountain speech in *outlander*, someone who's not from the local area

poll (n.)—the top of the head, a count of heads. See Numbers 1:18, 20, 22.

pottage (n.)—boiled food. This is, famously, what Jacob made and Esau bought with his birthright. See Genesis 25:29–34.

press (n. or v.)—crowd (not a group of reporters!), as in "When she had heard of Jesus, came in the press behind, and touched his garment" (Mark 5:27). Or, a machine that squeezes things (see Joel 3:13). Or, to urge forward, as in this single example, "I press toward the mark for the prize of the high calling of God in Christ Jesus" (Philippians 3:14).

publican (n.)—tax-collector (often corrupt in New Testament times)

pulse (n.)—don't let this one throw you: in its three instances in the KJV it doesn't have to do with blood circulation, but simply means "herbs" or "vegetables"

quick (adj. or n.)—alive or something living, as in "him that is ready to judge the quick and the dead" (1 Peter 4:5)

quit (v.)—to prove oneself or to clear oneself of further duty (as in *acquit*). "Then we will be quit of thine oath which thou hast made us to swear" (Joshua 2:20); or from Paul: "Watch ye, stand fast in the faith, quit you like men, be strong" (1 Corinthians 16:13).

quiver (n.)—a sheath for arrows. Made famous in recent days by the "Quiverful Movement," which teaches that Christians should eschew all birth control. They take as their inspiration, "As arrows are in the hand of a mighty man; so are children of the youth. Happy is the man that hath his quiver full of them" (Psalm 127:4–5).

rearward (n.)—In Isaiah 52:12 (repeated in the RV), this word means "the rear guard or an army," roughly equivalent to the English idiom, "I'll have your back"

reins (n.)—in archaic use literally meant "kidneys," but should be read not in the anatomical sense, but in the metaphorical sense akin to our expression, "She really showed some *heart*." Otherwise, how confusing Proverbs 23:16, "my reins shall rejoice"— would be! In eight out of the eighteen verses that use the word, "reins" occurs together with the word "heart." See Psalm 16:7, "I will bless the LORD, who hath given me counsel: my reins also instruct me in the night seasons." The word *kidneys* is most faithful to the original Hebrew, even though it can be confusing. NRSV and NIV render it as "heart."

rent (n.)—a breach or tear. Eighty-one times this little word appears, and in most cases it refers to clothes being torn. But there are other uses too, like this occasion when the prophet Samuel told King Saul that his royal days had come to an end: "The LORD hath rent the kingdom out of thine hand, and given it to thy neighbor, even to David" (1 Samuel 28:17).

repent (v.)—sometimes meant "regret," as in the description of God's feelings that led to the Flood: "It repented the LORD that he had made man on the earth, and it grieved him at his heart" (Genesis 6:6).

satyr (n.)—in mythology, a demigod creature that is half man, half goat. See Isaiah 13:21 and 34:14.

scrip (n.)—traveler's bag

secret parts (n.) — what we might idiomatically call "private parts," as in 1 Samuel 5:9

seemed to be somewhat — this unusual phrase occurs memorably only once, in Galatians 2:6, and means "influential." The NIV renders it "seemed to be important."

seethe (v.) — to boil (rather than being angry!), as in "Thou shalt not seethe a kid in its mother's milk" (Exodus 23:19)

selah (v.) — this fascinating word occurs a whopping seventy-one times in the Psalms and three in Habakkuk, and yet, no one can agree on what it means. It seems that it's the translation of two Hebrew words and that it's intended primarily as a musical direction, like a pause in the music of singing a psalm. This also means, that *selah* tells us to think before we move on, as in "The Lord of hosts is with us; the God of Jacob is our refuge. Selah" (Psalm 46:7).

shalt (v.) — the archaic second person singular present tense of *shall*. Compare these two statements of Peter: "Be it far from thee, Lord: this shall not be unto thee" (Matthew 16:22) with "Thou shalt never wash my feet" (John 13:8).

signet (n.) — ring used to make a seal

slept with his fathers — died

sons of God (n.) — a confusing phrase, since in Job 1:6 it means "angels," but in John 1:12 it refers to humans: "But as many as received him, to them gave he power to become the sons of God, even to them that believe on his name"

soothsay (v.) — an interesting word that appears nine times — interesting because it is used somewhat differently in Shakespeare, as in *Macbeth*, Act I, scene 2: "If I say sooth, I must report ..." where it means "speak truly." But "soothsayer" and "soothsaying" mean "one who claims to foretell the future" and "foretelling the future."

suffer (v.)—allow (not a punishment!), as in "Lord, suffer me first to go" (Matthew 8:21), or the idiomatic "suffer fools gladly" (2 Corinthians 11:19)

taches (pl. n.)—clasps, as in, "And thou shalt hang up the vail under the taches ..." (Exodus 26:33)

talebearer (n.)—a gossip or teller of secrets, as in "The words of a talebearer are as wounds" (Proverbs 18:8)

tarry (v.)—wait or stay behind

thee (pron.)—singular accusative of *thou*. We often confuse *thee, thou, thy,* and *thine* with formal, or respectful, forms of address—but they were not. Throughout the KJV these are simply the singular forms of the second person pronoun. Memorably, Jesus says to the devil in Luke 4:8, "Get thee behind me, Satan!"

thence (adv.)—from that place or time

thine (pron.)—possessive form of *thou. Thy* is the most common possessive form, but *thine* is used whenever it is followed by a word that starts with a vowel, as in "let not thine anger burn" (Genesis 44:18), a word that starts with an *h,* as in "anoint thine head" (Matthew 6:17), or when used alone to mean "yours," as in "thine is the kingdom ..." (Matthew 6:13).

thou (pron.)—the KJV's second person singular. Most famously in Psalm 23:4 with, "I will fear no evil: for thou art with me; thy rod and thy staff they comfort me." This verse is also a good example of the possessive form of this pronoun (see next entry).

thy (pron.)—possessive form of *thou;* equivalent to *your*

tires (pl. n.)—adornments or an ornamented headband

unction (n.)—anointing

undersetters (pl. n.)—a pedestal or support. This word appears four times, all in 1 Kings 7.

unstopped (prep.)—occurring only once, I like how this word is used to mean more than "opened"; it means "no longer closed":

"Then the eyes of the blind shall be opened, and the ears of the deaf shall be unstopped" (Isaiah 35:5).

usury (n.) — interest due on money lent

vail (n.) — curtain, as in "And thou shalt hang up the vail under the taches" (Exodus 26:33), or a face covering, as in "And till Moses had done speaking with them, he put a vail on his face" (Exodus 34:33)

verily (adv.) — truly; with confidence

verily, verily (adv.) — very truly!

victuals (n.) — food for human beings, as in "they may go into the villages, and buy themselves victuals" (Matthew 14:15)

virtue (n.) — strength or moral goodness. This word appears in six verses in the New Testament, three times to mean "strength," as in "And Jesus said, Somebody hath touched me: for I perceive that virtue is gone out of me" (Luke 8:46); and three times to mean "moral goodness" (see Philippians 4:8).

wag (v.) — to move back and forth

want (adj.) — lack, as in "I shall not want" (Psalm 23:1)

watching (v. or n.) — to stay awake, or the process of staying awake

whelps (pl. n.) — the offspring of any mammal. Used in this ominous Proverb: "Let a bear robbed of her whelps meet a man, rather than a fool in his folly" (17:12).

whence (adv.) — meaning "from what place," as when the rabbis in the synagogue said of Jesus, "Whence hath this man this wisdom?" (Matthew 13:54)

whensoever (adv.) — whenever

wherefore (adv.) — therefore, or so; often the equivalent of "given what you've just heard." Again, I fondly remember A. A. Milne's usage of KJV English — as in the way that Eeyore thinks about things: "Sometimes he thought sadly to himself, 'Why?' and sometimes he thought, 'Wherefore?' and sometimes he thought 'Inasmuch as which?'—and sometimes he didn't quite know what he *was* thinking about."

whilst (conj.)—still common in British English, as on the British Airways website when it reads, "Please wait whilst we check prices and availability ..."

whoso, or **whosoever** (pron.)—old form of our more simple "whoever," as in "For whosoever hath, to him shall be given" (Matthew 13:12)

withal (adv. or prep.)—in addition to; with. This little word confuses easily, and appears forty-one times.

woe (n. or interj.)—deep distress and misery, from the Old English. This word is more famous in Shakespeare than in the KJV. "O, woe is me, / To have seen what I have seen, see what I see!" (*Hamlet*, Act 3, scene 1). KJV example: "Woe is me, that I sojourn in Mesech, that I dwell in the tents of Kedar!" (Psalm 120:5). "Woe unto you" is a phrase used by Jesus eight times in Matthew 23:13–29, as he reproves the Pharisees. Means "misfortune."

ye (pron.)—the nominative plural form of the second person (*you*), as in "Ye are the salt of the earth" (Matthew 5:13)

yea (adv. or n.)—yes; a yes vote. As Jesus said about the importance of clarity in life: "But let your communication be, Yea, yea; Nay, nay: for whatsoever is more than these cometh of evil" (Matthew 5:37).

yesternight (n.)—last night

zeal (n.)—an earnest emotion that can be enlightened (2 Corinthians 7:11) but also misguided or arrogant, driving the will, as when Paul remembers his former life: "Concerning zeal, persecuting the church" (Philippians 3:6), or in Romans 10:2, "For I bear them record that they have a zeal of God, but not according to knowledge."

ARCHAIC FORMS OF VERBS

The verb forms of the KJV—which are often the first thing that makes us feel distant from this beautiful translation—are actually quite easy to grasp. They follow a simple, consistent pattern.

+ The–st endings are used with the second person singular (*thou*) for most verbs: "Thou lovest righteousness" (Psalm 45:7).

+ The–th endings are used for the third person singular (*he*, *she*, or *it*): "For he that loveth his life shall lose it" (John 12:25).

+ The first person singular (*I*), and *all* of the plural pronouns (*we*, *ye* [since the KJV never uses *you* as the subject of a sentence], and *they*) are exactly the same as our modern English forms:

   "The world may know that I love the Father" (John 14:31)—first person singular

   "We know that we love the children of God" (1 John 5:2)—first person plural

   "If ye love them which love you" (Matthew 5:46)— second person plural

   "They love to pray standing in the synagogues" (Matthew 6:5)—third person plural

It's no more complicated than that; the other verb forms are pretty similar to modern English. There are a few exceptions to the rules, as always, the main ones being the verb *to be*, the second person singular of which is *thou art*, and the auxiliary verb *shall*, the second person singular of which is *thou shalt*.

Still, even *thou art* should be familiar to most people because of its use in the great hymn "How Great Thou Art," which, along with "Amazing Grace," is consistently voted as a favorite hymn of Christians in both the United States and the United Kingdom.

WORKS FREQUENTLY CONSULTED

PHYSICAL BOOKS

Ackroyd, Peter. *Albion: The Origins of the English Imagination.* New York: Anchor Books, 2004.

————. *The Life of Thomas More.* New York: Doubleday, 1998.

Beer, Anna. *Milton: Poet, Pamphleteer, and Patriot.* New York: Bloomsbury Press, 2008.

Bobrick, Benson. *Wide as the Waters: The Story of the English Bible and the Revolution It Inspired.* New York: Simon & Schuster, 2001.

Callahan, Allen Dwight. *The Talking Book: African Americans and the Bible.* New Haven: Yale University Press, 2006.

Carter, John and Percy H. Muir. *Printing and the Mind of Man: A Descriptive Catalogue Illustrating the Impact of Print on the Evolution of Western Civilization During Five Centuries.* New York: Holt, Rinehart and Winston, 1967.

Daniell, David. *Tyndale's New Testament.* New Haven: Yale University Press, 1989.

————. *Tyndale's Old Testament.* New Haven: Yale University Press, 1992.

Davies, Donald, ed. *The Psalms in English.* New York: Penguin Books, 1996.

De Hamel, Christopher. *The Book: A History of the Bible*. New York: Phaidon Press, 2001.

Ferrell, Lori Anne. *The Bible and the People*. New Haven: Yale University Press, 2008.

Hoffman, Joel M. *And God Said: How Translations Conceal the Bible's Original Meaning*. New York: St. Martin's Press, 2010.

Johnson, Samuel. *A Dictionary of the English Language: An Anthology*, ed. by David Crystal. New York: Penguin Books, 2006.

Kaplan, Fred. *Lincoln: The Biography of a Writer*. New York: HarperCollins, 2008.

McGrath, Alister E. *In the Beginning: The Story of the King James Bible and How It Changed a Nation, a Language, and a Culture*. New York: Doubleday, 2001.

Milne, A. A. *Winnie-the-Pooh*, with decorations by Ernest H. Shepard. London: Methuen and Company, 1926.

Nicolson, Adam. *God's Secretaries: The Making of the King James Bible*. New York: HarperCollins, 2003.

Thuesen, Peter J. *In Discordance with the Scriptures: American Protestant Battles over Translating the Bible*. New York: Oxford University Press, 1999.

Washington, James Melvin, ed. *A Testament of Hope: The Essential Writings and Speeches of Martin Luther King Jr.* New York: HarperOne, 1990.

Weir, Alison. *The Six Wives of Henry VIII*. New York: Ballantine Books, 1993.

EBOOKS AND ONLINE RESOURCES

There are multiple electronic and online KJVs available, iPhone/iPad applications, and more on the way. In the future, as printings of physical editions fade, I imagine that these highly accessible, affordable, searchable, portable options will be what truly keeps the Authorized Version alive.

Bible Gateway has a tremendous KJV online Bible: *www.biblegateway.com*. You can easily look up passages and compare them between various languages and other English translations (including the NIV, The Message, New American Standard Bible, Wycliffe's New Testament, and many others). You can also set up a daily reading plan for yourself (available via email, RSS, and iCal), making it easy to read through the entire KJV, through daily installments, over the course of a year. There are other plans, as well. I also find its topical index helpful.

In addition, I've appreciated the exhaustive concordance and dictionary found in these:

+ *www.artbible.info/* created and maintained by contentecontent.com, an Internet publisher based in Amsterdam, the Netherlands. This site reproduces classic paintings and links them to stories/passages from the KJV. Their concordance to the 1611 KJV is excellent.
+ *www.av1611.com* offers a dictionary to all of the words in the 1611 KJV (as do a few other sites). This site also includes an online version of the KJV, indexed by chapter.

And then I enjoy the online parallel Bible features at Biblos: *www.bible.cc*. You can search by passage or verse and up comes the KJV in a vertical column together with the same passage or verse in more than a dozen other translations, past and present, and below them, selections from prominent and historical commentators on that passage.